Scott Reeves is the author of *Gold Top: The John Lund Story* and
Keep Turning Left. He has been a keen stock car fan
since his first trip to Odsal Stadium in 1987.

KINGS OF THE OVAL

Scott Reeves

Foreword by John Lund

Chequered Flag
PUBLISHING

Published in the UK by Chequered Flag Publishing
PO Box 4669, Sheffield, S6 9ET
www.chequeredflagpublishing.co.uk

A CIP record for this book is available from the British Library

ISBN 9780993215216

Printed and bound in the UK by Henry Ling Limited

Picture acknowledgements
Mike Greenwood, Photostox: pp ii, 12, 13, 24, 25, 34, 73, 110, 117
Scott Reeves: pp opp i, 14, 39
Kevin Wickham: p 122
All other images courtesy Colin Casserley, stoxphotos.com

Dedicated to Theo van Lier
and the drivers and safety crew who saved his life

CONTENTS

FOREWORD

53

JOHN LUND

I've been in Formula 1 stock cars for almost forty years. My first meeting was on Sunday 28 March at Rochdale. Things were quite different back then!

Tracks were more local. If you lived in Huddersfield, you could race in Nelson, Rochdale, Bradford and Blackburn without travelling for more than an hour. A working man could do it; he could still go to work and then set off with his car for the racetrack. If you were a plumber you could finish a job at five and then be at Nelson by six. Then you'd stop off in the pub on the way home!

Although there were a lot of good drivers when I started, not many of them had competitive cars. Drivers would build their own cars and the only way to make them quicker was to do something in your own workshop. You would have to make your own parts or alter something yourself if you wanted to make it better, so there were lots of slower cars and the track would get blocked so you'd have to bash your way through.

There was still some science to it though, especially with tyres. They were all old cross-plys and quite a lot of them were second-hand ones that came off road cars. A lot of it was about preparing your tyres on shale for tarmac. You'd run a tyre on shale for two or three races to get it just right for tarmac.

The results didn't matter as much because it didn't cost so much to go racing. You were doing it more for a laugh.

Now, things are very different. The biggest change is that you've got to spend so much time travelling to race regularly. Now it takes four hours to get to the

Racing since 1976, Lund has worn the gold roof eight times...

track and costs a fortune in diesel. The lads who can operate their own businesses and get time off easily are in a better position. You didn't have that before. It becomes a bit more serious. You have more pressure to do well when you get there because it takes a lot more effort.

Also, the cars are better. They have become lighter but they are still as strong. Everybody goes quicker and the racing is much faster and more exciting, but because everybody is going at the same speed, it's more difficult to pass them. You have to be much more like a racing car driver, much smoother, you have to make up the ground in other ways. Car setup is more important now than it ever was. You're looking for that tiny bit extra all the time, particularly on tarmac, your car has to be spot on, especially because everybody is on the same tyres as well.

There are probably more good drivers because a lot of them have been racing Ministox since they were ten. They've learned track craft and got experience, so when they get into a Formula 1 at seventeen or eighteen, they're up and running straight away. Frankie Wainman Junior, Paul Harrison and Rob Speak were probably the first ones to come through, but a lot have raced since and many of the ones who have carried on have become top drivers.

Some people might think that it would be better to go back to how racing was when I first started, but it's difficult to go backwards once you've moved forwards. It's not just the car specifications – you can't take the knowledge away. Over the

...and he still gets stuck in as he approaches four full decades in stock car racing

years, everybody has gained knowledge about how to set cars up, what works and what doesn't work. You can alter the car specification and say "you can't use these shockers" and "you must use these tyres" but because the drivers know what makes the car go faster, they'll work around it. But you've got to be careful that it doesn't become too expensive by having too many expensive bolt-on parts that you've got to have to be quick.

How good is the current generation of drivers? It's difficult to say. I don't think you could bring the drivers who used to do well in the seventies into the modern day and expect them to do so well. Some would, but a lot would struggle, because the car setup is so different. But drivers who have come into the sport more recently, they'd all have adapted pretty quickly if they had been racing with me in the late seventies. Dan Johnson, Mat Newson, Tom Harris: they'd all go well round Rochdale or Nelson in 1976!

Formula 1 stock cars is looking good for the future. When Ministox are racing at the same meetings as Formula 1, the amount of interest from the young ones is good. The boys and girls who race in Minis, their mates who come to watch, they're all interested. Hopefully they will carry on and stay involved as they get older. In the early nineties, I felt that there weren't too many young ones among the spectators. A lot of the fans were hanging on from the sixties and seventies. A lot of the drivers went as the tracks fizzled out. When Bradford went, we lost a lot of drivers from the Huddersfield and Bradford area. When Hartlepool and Aycliffe went, we lost a lot of drivers from the North-East. But we seem to have got through that now. There are some good, young drivers coming through like Will Hunter.

I keep racing because of the people, mainly. The spectators, other drivers and their families – a lot of them I've known for forty years! I've raced with the fathers of many of the current drivers. I knew Stuart Smith Junior and Craig Finnikin when they were babies!

It's a family thing, too. The girls enjoy going, so do Annette and her dad. It's a good way to spend a Saturday night – meet up with friends and do a bit of racing. I enjoy it. Obviously I'm going to have to stop sometime, but I'm not planning on it just yet. As long as I can be on the same lap as the majority of people and so long as my body keeps together, I'll be there!

John Lund

World Champion
1987, 1988, 1991, 1992, 1996, 1997, 2000, 2002

National Points Champion
1987, 1988, 1989, 1990, 1991, 1992

British Champion
1987, 1989, 1990, 1995, 1997, 1998

European Champion
1989, 1992, 2002

UK OPEN CHAMPION

390

STUART SMITH JUNIOR

Sunday 11 May 2014. A typical spring day in Skegness: damp and slightly chilly.

27 BriSCA Formula 1 stock cars slowly edge around the oval racetrack. The calm before the storm. As the lead cars come in sight of the starter, he waves a green flag – the signal for fury to be unleashed. 27 race-tuned V8 engines roar, 108 tyres squeal as they fight for grip on the tarmac. 54 steel bumpers are about to be tested.

Will Hunter leads as he rounds the first corner from pole position, his wheels slightly mounting the inside kerb as he tries to avoid being hit by the cars behind. Hunter's yellow roof indicates that he is one of the drivers eligible to start towards the front of the grid, a handicap designed to level the playing field. Less experienced drivers have as much chance of winning as those with a proven record of success.

Behind Hunter and the small pack of yellow tops comes the next grade of drivers with a blue roof. Their better results means that they start further back, although if they are to make progress they must first escape the melee of clashing wheels and metal bumpers. On the second lap, two blue tops find themselves being shoved wide and hit the Armco fence hard. One of them rolls to a halt at the end of the turn, wheels turned in to the fence, a vulnerable sitting duck.

Piling into the stranded car from behind is one of the best drivers, owning the right to race with the red roof and flashing amber lights of a superstar: Frankie Wainman Junior. If Wainman wants to win this race, he will have to do it the hard

You're going the wrong way! SSJ gets in trouble during the UK Open heats...

way – by passing nearly every car starting in front of him. Such is the lot of the superstar, but he has done it plenty of times before.

Not today. Wainman is forced to reverse back from the stalled car while the rest of the field floods past him. Already he has been left with too much to do. The 45th title of Wainman's long and successful career will have to wait until another day.

Yellow flags are waved, bringing the cars to a temporary halt. Once the stranded blue top is safely removed to the centre green, racing restarts. Drivers jostle for position and other cars hit the fence, this time only suffering glancing blows. Among them is Paul Harrison, his number 2 a familiar sight on the track for almost three decades. Harrison was helped on his way by the front bumper of Rob Speak. It's not the first or last time that Speak will put an opponent in the fence.

With half the race gone and a dry racing line now visible, the front runners are established and the red tops are working their way through the field. Mat Newson has made his way into first place, a blistering start aiding his way through the blues and yellows. Tom Harris lurks nearby, gold roof betraying his presence to all around him. There's no hiding when you're the World Champion.

Five laps to go and Newson braces himself. Bearing down upon him is the ominous sight of Stuart Smith Junior's car. Smith times his attack perfectly and pushes Newson wide into a yellow top in the wrong place at the wrong time – or

KINGS OF THE OVAL

...but recovers to take the chequered flag and the first championship of the season

the right place at the right time – allowing Smith to accelerate into the lead down the straight.

Newson is forced to defend second position from Harris and Speak, both sniffing around like hyenas looking to take advantage of a lion's kill. Smith pulls a few car-lengths into the lead and takes the chequered flag for victory. The first championship of the sixtieth season of BriSCA Formula 1 Stock Cars – the UK Open Championship – belongs to Stuart Smith Junior.

"I didn't feel ecstatic when I went over the line, it wasn't spectacular. I was a bit surprised," Smith admits. "I got a bit worried about that. When I've won a championship before it has been an unbelievable feeling, the best feeling in the world, but I think I'd had too many life experiences in the previous years. I'd realised there is more to life than stock cars."

Smith had been through a few tough years and his victory at the UK Open saw him re-emerging from a dark period. The death of his father just before Christmas 2010 created upheaval in more ways than one. Stuart Smith Senior had created a successful business which suddenly fell on the shoulders of Stuart Junior and his older brother, Andrew. Stuart Senior was also the most successful stock car racing driver the sport had ever known and the lynchpin around which his sons' racing careers revolved. With him gone, Andrew's desire waned and he retired from the sport at the end of 2011, moving away from his homeland and leaving the business in Stuart's hands. Stuart Junior was also struggling to stay motivated to race, but if truth be told, it had started before his father's passing.

"I last properly raced in 2009," Smith explains. "After that season I felt burnt out. 2010 was a bit of a bad year. New Goodyear tyres came in and I struggled with them and it put me off. I started seeing my future wife and my dad died. I decided then to back away from racing. After 2011 I decided to have a couple of years off. I half raced in 2012 but it was a real half-arsed approach and didn't really go that well. In 2013 I totally had a year off."

There were fears among fans that the Smith family, inextricably linked to Formula 1 stock cars for nearly fifty years, would permanently vanish from the sport. That was never Stuart's intention. Although he was not racing, he could often be found in the garage, building two new stock cars. It was as though he wanted to wipe the slate clean and start afresh. His new shale car was completed a couple of months into the season, but it was on tarmac that Smith would make his comeback, fighting for the UK Open Championship. That meant using his old tarmac car, seven years old and anything but clean and fresh.

"You can never ever be at the top when you get a car out of the back of the bus that you haven't raced properly for three years," Smith explains. "You have to spend quite a lot of time on it, and we did. We stripped it down and took it to bits. Didn't renovate it, just did the fundamentals – made sure that the clutch, axles and suspension were right, put new shockers on, the new American Racer tyres. I knew that we would go to Skegness and be fast. You don't forget how to be fast and what it feels like. The only concern that I had was that everybody else would have an advantage on car setup and the new shockers and tyres. Other people had had a good two months on them before the UK Open."

The initial signs were not promising, but things soon improved.

"I went out in practice on Saturday and it was horrendous. It was the worst car I have ever driven! But we eventually got it right and on the Saturday night it was really quick, just as quick as everybody else. I set the second-fastest lap time that night. In the final I was tailing Tom Harris and Rob Speak and I felt quicker than them. It was no surprise to me that I was on the pace. I've always been on the pace. You don't just lose it overnight. I think everybody else was a bit more surprised. Coming up to the championship, I don't think anybody gave me a chance. I was considered to be some kind of has-been. It's surprising how people think of you when you've been away for just twelve months or a couple of years. But I knew that I would have a go. I took a lot of confidence from being quick on Saturday night."

Weekend meetings present a specific set of challenges to stock car drivers. Drivers race on Saturday evening under floodlights. The air temperature gradually cools, particularly in spring and summer. The next morning, conditions can be completely different. This time, the track is slowly warming. The weather might have completely changed overnight. Setup almost has to start from scratch.

"Going into the next day, in different conditions, is something I've always struggled a little bit with," Smith reveals. "You have to second-guess what changes you have to make. Believe it or not, stock cars are quite technical these days; you do have to think about stuff like that! We tried a few things as well to make the car better, mainly to do with tyres, but we went backwards."

Smith lined up on the outside of the seventh row. He was in front of the superstars – Tom Harris, Mat Newson, Rob Speak and Frankie Wainman Junior among them – but still in the midst of some great drivers.

"It was damp but starting to dry out. I don't mean to blow my own trumpet but I've always believed I'm a good driver in tricky conditions, when you have to read how much grip you have. You can't just spin your wheels and hope you go fast. I can feed the power on and feel the drive underneath me."

Coping in the wet is a sign of the best drivers: Ayrton Senna, Gilles Villeneuve and Stirling Moss were among those who excelled in wet conditions.

"I wouldn't put myself in that category!" Smith laughs. "But it's the same with dry shale. I like it when it's really slick. It takes quite a lot to be disciplined when you race on those sorts of tracks. The UK Open was that sort of race. I had to be so gingerish with the throttle on the corners. Imagine you have the sort of grip that a pushbike has got in the wet, only with 700 brake horsepower. It's ridiculous really, the amount of horsepower we've got in those conditions. You don't need it. You could probably put a Mini engine in and you'd be alright!"

Smith had a good start and progressed quickly to the top three, but wasn't able to stop Mat Newson getting past him.

"Mat was going well. I've been in a few close races with him; he was winning the World Final that I won in 2007 too. He deserved both those races, but I caught him with two to go and luckily for me everything went alright and I won the race."

It was the fifth title in a racing career which, although not flush with success, has seen Smith win three of the major championships: World, British and National Points. Yet it's surprising that, given his high-profile father, Stuart Junior was initially not keen to take after him.

"When I was ten years old, I had a go in a Ministox. It was just expected. I didn't get bullied into it; I got gently nudged in that direction. But I just didn't like it. It wasn't for me. I didn't bother after that. I only did seven meetings and I wasn't very good – pretty rubbish really. I thought I would never race again. I started helping my brother Andrew when I was twelve or thirteen, being a mechanic, getting involved with setup. I really enjoyed that side of it and didn't have any aspirations to drive myself."

Things began to change after a few years.

"The first time I ever thought I'd like to have a go at it myself was in the mid-nineties when I was about fourteen. I remember watching Andrew and John Lund at Bradford, watching them drift around the big wide corners, and I thought it must be fun. On my sixteenth birthday, Andrew and his wife Lisa bought me a one-meeting drive in a Rebel. I was nervous as hell. I did feel a bit of pressure. When I jumped in I thought people would be watching me but they weren't. My first race was clutch start, like all Rebel races are. I was right at the back. When I let the clutch out, I went backwards! I had it in reverse! I couldn't get it in first gear. I got pummelled onto the infield and then eventually got going when I found first gear. I kind of enjoyed it but I just thought it was a one-off thing. After that Anthony Flanagan let me have a go in his Formula 2. Again, I didn't do much but I showed little signs of being able to control the car. Then I got offered a V8 Hotstox and it snowballed from there."

Smith made his V8 Hotstox debut in 2000 and quickly rose to be one of the top drivers in the formula, winning the right to wear both the gold and silver roof. V8 Hotstox was gaining a reputation as a training ground for drivers who would ultimately transfer to Formula 1 – Smith's own brother Andy had done just that – and fans were waiting expectantly for Stuart Junior to follow.

"It happened one day in 2001," Smith remembers, "there was a F1 meeting at Northampton which Andrew was booked into but he just didn't fancy racing. He said to me, 'do you want to race tonight?' So we organised it all on the day and I had a go in Andrew's car. The first couple of races I just got used to it, the power and the weight more than anything, they are quite heavy things. I did OK and qualified for the final. Andrew bolted some new tyres on, I think he'd put on some right old crappers for the heats because he didn't know how I would go. In the final I nearly won, John Lund passed me with one lap to go. I tried a last bender on him but it didn't go to plan and I came second. To nearly win your first final in Formula 1 is quite a feat, but nobody remembers nearly."

The clamour for Smith to move full-time to Formula 1 only grew after that first performance, but he kept fans waiting a little longer.

"I'd shown that I could have a decent future in Formula 1 if I did choose to go into it, but I didn't for another couple of years. When I did, I didn't start until part way through the season because I was building a new car."

Smith's initial drives in Ministox, Rebels and Formula 2 had been fairly plain affairs, but his years in V8 Hotstox had honed him into a true racing driver. By the time he moved into Formula 1, he was ready to hit the ground running. He won his first meeting final at the fourth time of asking, qualified on the fifth row for the World Final and on the third row in the British Championship.

Smith's first meeting final win – Belle Vue, June 2003

The pressure of expectation on Smith because of his illustrious surname was huge. Not only was he a son of the great Stuart Senior, but Andy won the gold and silver roofs during Stuart's first few seasons in F1 – a fact that he was keen to point out to his little brother.

"I was always chasing a championship. I remember Andrew saying to me, 'if you don't win a championship soon you might as well pack in!'"

Andy's ribbing was good-natured, but there was little doubt that the pressure was real. It not only came from the weight of expectation. Much of it was self-imposed.

"If I didn't win, I didn't enjoy it," Stuart explains. "I'd wish I hadn't gone. I'd wish I hadn't bothered. And that's unhealthy really. I was doing a lot of the work myself and I was working on the cars nearly every night during the week."

Smith picked up a reputation for liberal use of the bumper. He would hit hard – sometimes a little too hard – and ask questions later. No problem with that, stock car racing is contact motorsport after all, but Smith would occasionally allow his frustration to get the better of him.

Of course, it helped gain a few good results. Five seasons in, Smith landed that elusive first title. And he started with the biggest prize the sport had to offer – the World Championship, held at King's Lynn in 2007.

The coveted gold roof – Smith racing in his year as World Champion

"I had a sick engine which had to be rebuilt pretty quickly," Smith recalls. "We finally got the engine in the car around 3 o'clock on the morning of the World Final."

Sitting pretty in pole position was Andy Smith, the pre-race favourite, reigning World Champion and National Points Champion. Alongside him was the British Champion, Frankie Wainman Junior – if anybody would beat Andy, surely it could only be him. However, stock car racing is unpredictable and nothing can be taken for granted.

"There was one moment which was crucial and determined the end of the race," Stuart says. "About seven laps in, Andrew was leading. I was second and Frankie was third. I knew that Frankie wouldn't be able to resist taking us both out! I positioned my car so Andrew took the full brunt of it. To be honest, I did go for Andrew a little bit myself because he was the quickest man on the day."

The result was that Mat Newson took the lead while Stuart stayed in second and Wainman in third. The big loser was Andy, who was stuck on a parked car.

"I couldn't see anybody in my mirror but I could see Mat in front. Eventually I caught Mat and passed him. Then Frankie started to catch me again towards the end of the race. I was taking it too easy. I'd always had nightmares about leading the World Final then doing something stupid like spinning out! I knew that

Frankie was going to have a go on the last corner so I positioned my car so if I did get hit it wouldn't affect me."

Smith crossed the finish line in front of Wainman with less than a second to spare.

"The win that has meant the most to me by a country mile is the World Championship," Stuart says, "but the one where I achieved more was the Shootout in 2009. It's a lot harder to win; there are more competitors who are eligible for it."

Add in the British Championship in 2008 and Smith had a glorious three years in which he won three major championships. It was a period when the Smith brothers dominated – Andy won the other two World and British titles in the same years.

But it hit hard when Stuart Senior, the larger-than-life figurehead of Team Smith, died in 2010. The Smith family's world collapsed around them. Thankfully, four years on, the hurt has healed and Stuart Junior announced his return in spectacular fashion at the UK Open.

"It was success straight away, but I couldn't kid myself and think I had it cracked," Smith explains. "I still had to work hard on the set up of the car. But a couple of Andrew's old mechanics and a couple of new mechanics meant that I had a really good team around me. I could relax more. The rest of the season went alright. I can't really complain."

Two weeks after the UK Open triumph, Smith unveiled his quirky new shale car with its distinctive high wing and short nose. It helped him to second place in his first meeting final and won the meeting final at Coventry two weeks after that.

"I put a lot of effort into building the new car," Smith reveals. "I had a few ideas and put them into practice and ended up with a car that looks quite different. The new wing – well, there was a bit of philosophy about it. I think the wing is better than a sloper, but you'll never know, we don't have sensors all over the car to test it to know whether it is any better or not, you can only put it on and see. You can't get sideways in a wind tunnel! But it was also to do with looks. It's good to build something that doesn't look like just another Tom Harris or Frankie Wainman Junior build."

Smith has always built his own cars. It certainly helped having a guiding hand from his brother and top constructor Stephen 'Cecil' Sayers. Is it a good thing, not relying on other car builders?

"One hundred percent," Stuart answers. "It always used to be like that. The top lads would always build their own cars. Now there are four or five people building cars professionally and it's difficult to compete with them. If it's your hobby, it will always come second. To compete against those lads you have to sacrifice quite a lot, and that tends to be giving up time with your family and business."

Following a good debut, the shale car got better and better as the season went on. But it was the opposite with the old tarmac car. Having won the UK Open, things gradually deteriorated.

"The tarmac car was a bit of a disaster really. There was a little problem with the engine – it was blowing water out – and we couldn't for the life of us find out why."

In midsummer, the sickly engine meant that Smith faced a dilemma. Should he push to get into the top twelve in the National Points Championship to qualify for the Shootout and the race for the silver roof, or should he play it safe and concentrate on the World Championship?

"There was a bit of a debate in the workshop whether to swop the engines between the cars to make sure I always had the good engine in," Smith reveals. "That would mean I could go for the silver roof. But we didn't have the time to do the swops and we still wanted to keep the tarmac engine in the tarmac car because we wanted to find out what the problem was and solve it. And I had the semi-final to think of because I drew the tarmac World Semi-Final at Skegness. We did a lot of work, focusing just on that one race. We took the engine out and did some tests, had it stripped down and rebuilt. We thought we'd cured it but it was pretty evident straight away at Skegness that it hadn't. I decided to do the semi-final and then load up because it wasn't worth doing more damage."

Concentrating on getting the tarmac car right for the World Semi-Final probably cost Smith vital points and meant that he pulled up short in his attempt to qualify for the Shootout. If he had qualified, the chances are that he would have been a front runner for the silver roof. The new shale car hit peak form and Smith was unstoppable. Of the four Shootout rounds that he competed in, Smith won five races, two of which were meeting finals, and gained four other podium places. Yes, he was starting a grade in front of the Shootout drivers, but such was his domination of those meetings that it's likely he would have picked up race wins even if he had been starting with the drivers competing in the Shootout.

It's all hypothetical. Smith wasn't in the Shootout, but he did finish the season on a high. The signs are promising for the future. His personal life is settled. He's got to grips with running his own business. He's back racing properly. And he still knows how to use the bumper. Surely he's set for a long career in Formula 1 stock cars?

"I have actually thought about that a lot recently," Smith says. "I've just had a little boy. I've thought about how long I want to race for and what I want to achieve. I want to win the World Championship again. I don't want to be known as a one-hit wonder. Once isn't enough in this family, they tend to win it five or six times! But to be regarded as one of the top lads who have been involved in the sport – that will be enough for me."

No mistaking this car! Smith's distinctive new look on shale.

The returning Stuart Smith Junior has also noticed that he is getting a little more love from the terraces.

"I don't think I can say that I've ever been a popular driver. I've always been a marmite sort of driver. Love me or hate me. People used to think that I was too hard or a bit miserable. But since returning I've had loads of support."

But the biggest difference since he returned to the racetrack is that the pressure and weight of expectation in carrying the Smith name seems to have dissolved.

"I've already achieved enough to prove to people that I can drive," Smith explains. "I think I'm a good driver. The only pressure I have now is to make other people happy: the fans; the lads who are involved; my wife, who loves racing. I want to have a good time and to enjoy it. It's brilliant when you win and go and have a drink afterwards. Those are the moments that you cherish. That's what I want to achieve rather than the status as World Champion. That's the right way to look at it."

The Maestro

It's hardly surprising that expectations were high when a second Stuart Smith took to the racetrack. After all, the first of that name won pretty much everything that could be won in stock car racing: three-times British Champion, six-times World Champion and thirteen-times National Points Champion. He finished his career with exactly 500 meeting final wins, a record never likely to be eclipsed. Unfortunately, they were successes that his son was too young to see with his own eyes.

"My first memory I have of watching my dad race was in a V8 Hotstox at Belle Vue after he had retired from Formula 1."

Even so, it didn't take much to become aware that his dad was something special behind the wheel.

"He had a one-off go in an F1 at Bolton in Mike James' car. I remember feeling nervous for the first time when watching somebody – I'd never seen my dad race properly! I also saw him win a veterans race one year in my brother's car. He had never sat in it until he drove around on the rolling lap. He just jumped straight in; never spun it out, never overcooked it. You start to believe the hype and history of what he achieved and how good he was to be able to do that. I've jumped in other peoples' cars and struggled a bit – it's hard work. Dad had a go in my car at

Peter Falding's testimonial and famously won that and lapped me. I was the current World Champion at that time. Things like that have brought home to me how good he was."

Having the best driver in the history of the sport as part of your team should have been a real asset. But, Stuart Junior reveals, that wasn't necessarily the case!

"He very much let me do whatever I wanted to do. He would say if he thought I was really wrong but he wouldn't tell me how to do things. He'd suggest ten inches of stagger and old-fashioned ideas like that. Generally we'd all tell him to shut up!"

NOVICE OF THE YEAR

220
WILL HUNTER

Each year, a handful of drivers nervously edge their stock car on track for the first time. Taking a place on a grid with up to thirty other unlimited horsepower, custom-built racing machines takes a huge amount of grit and bravery.

This is oval motorsport's premier formula. Few buckle themselves in to a Formula 1 stock car without first gaining experience of oval racing elsewhere. Most have raced in Ministox, a junior formula for eleven to fifteen year olds, where kids can learn driving skills and how to take contact. Some come from other senior formula – Formula 2, V8 Hotstox, grasstrack – gradually building up the power and speed until they are ready for the big league.

Frankie Wainman Junior and Paul Harrison cut their teeth in Ministox. Rob Speak spent a decade dominating Formula 2. Stuart Smith Junior was a successful V8 Hotstox racer. Yet Will Hunter found himself on a different path, one that was leading him to the other kind of Formula 1.

"I started in karts when I was seven or eight," Hunter reveals. "There's a local indoor karting track at Burscough that I used to go to. I was quite fast, so I decided I wanted to have a go more seriously. I started in Cadets with a little 50cc Honda, and then worked my way up over seven years to Senior Rotax Max at British and European level."

Although Hunter was building a name for himself on the circuits, following the path taken by Nigel Mansell and Lewis Hamilton among many others, his father had a different kind of motorsport pedigree. Warren Hunter raced Formula

1 stock cars for five years in the early nineties, a consistent red top who appeared in two World Finals and finished just off the podium in a World Championship Semi-Final and the UK Open Championship.

"He stopped when I was born," Hunter explains. "He used to talk about it and we would watch videos every now and again of his World Finals. But the karting distracted us from it. My dad was happy for me to start karting instead of stock cars. He likes being around racing, any kind of motorsport, and liked setting up the kart and mechanicing as much as he did driving. He was there every weekend. Karting meetings took place from Friday evening, all day Saturday and all day Sunday, so we didn't get time to go to stock cars."

After eight years or so, karting was beginning to get to Hunter, both physically and psychologically. Driving the kart was causing chronic compartment syndrome in his arms – cramping caused by restricted blood flow. Racing was becoming painful and less enjoyable. Hunter decided to call time on his promising karting career. Suddenly, weekends were free again and Hunter senior was able to take Hunter junior to view the motorsport in which he once took a part.

"The first stock car meeting that I went to was the World Championship that Paul Harrison won at Northampton in 2011. I was seventeen. I thought no, that's not for me, it was way too intimidating!"

Will wasn't ready to make the jump to contact racing. Yet.

"I didn't go at all the following year. Then, when I was nineteen, we started going to more meetings and I wanted to have a go. My dad still knew quite a lot of people who had been around while he was racing in the nineties. We went to speak to Frankie Wainman Junior first, and we spoke to Paul Harrison, but they didn't have anything going. We were put us in touch with Dave Johnson, who was selling James Waters' cars for him. So we went to a test day at Northampton, Dan Johnson came down with the car for us, and I really liked it. Then we didn't know what to do – whether to hire a car or buy one. We went to see James Waters about his tarmac car, just to start with. Then about two or three weeks later we had both cars and the wagon from him. We jumped in at the deep end! But I'm glad we did it. Getting both cars and the wagon in one go was the best thing to do from a cost point-of-view because they were good cars."

Hunter had all the gear, but not really any idea of how to use it properly. One of the toughest experiences in motorsport was about to begin – his first race in stock car racing. Contact was not just allowed, it was encouraged. It was going to be quite different from anything he had done before.

Hunter raced two meetings towards the end of the 2013 season, both on the Birmingham tarmac, both starting from the back of the grid with a large black X on the back of his car. He was a novice driver. Starting at the back gave him a

Everybody has to start somewhere – the white roof of the beginner driver

chance to take a few corners without the rest of the field on his back bumper, the X marking him out as a driver who should be given a little leeway by the others.

"It's an incredible feeling when you go out for the first time," Hunter says. "Testing is one thing. When you're on a track on your own, it's easy really, but when you're on a track and there are thirty others, it's just a completely different thing. It was just pure intimidation – not so much when you start at the back, but after a few laps when you've got a car on your back bumper, on a restart or something."

Hunter's results were spectacularly unspectacular in his two Birmingham try-outs. He earned two top ten finishes – creeping over the line in tenth in his first race, improving by one to finish ninth in the second meeting final.

It was quite a change. Hunter was used to visiting the Birmingham Wheels complex so he could drive on the karting circuit, not on the oval.

"They are different in every way possible," Hunter explains. "Karting is all about speed and pace. There's no advantage with contact – it's actually a disadvantage because if you hit somebody you're out. It was very hard to get to the high level that I was at in karting. It's unbelievably precise – you're talking degrees on the steering wheel and things like that. Stock car racing is far more brutal and a lot more intimidating. You get away with some things. You don't have to be perfect,

Moving up the grades and starting further back didn't stop Hunter

you're turning left all the time, there's not so much to learn, but the biggest difference is how much more intimidating and brutal it is, and the power."

Hunter had a huge learning curve, one made even steeper given the fact that stock car drivers have to learn to race on two different surfaces. Come the inaugural meeting of the 2014 season, he rolled out on track for his third-ever meeting – his last with the option of starting at the back of the grid as a novice – on the shale at Belle Vue Stadium.

"When I first went on shale, that was completely different again," Hunter remembers. "I had no idea how to do it! My dad said what it would be like and how I would have to play with the throttle, but without ever going out and trying it, you'll never know. It looks easier than it actually is, you think 'I can drift like that', but when you have 600 horsepower underneath it really is quite difficult!"

Just as at Birmingham, Hunter began the meeting in fairly unspectacular fashion.

"I remember going out in the first heat and my car wasn't set up. I hadn't adjusted the brakes because I didn't know where they should be and I couldn't quite get the hang of playing on the throttle and the brakes. I wasn't very good in the first heat and I think I got lapped by everyone. In the second heat, I got a bit of a better start and I was getting used to it, but I didn't expect to do anything in the meeting final."

For the first time, Hunter was about to do something on track that would cause spectators to take notice of the newcomer.

"I set off from the back and I was driving a lot better than I had done in the first two heats. There were quite a few crashes but I don't think there were any yellow flags. I kept going through crash after crash after crash. I was getting better and better and was really improving fast. I came up behind Nigel Harrhy with a couple of laps to go. Danny Wainman was behind me. He was catching ever so slowly, I thought he would be catching faster, so I knew I must be going alright. Danny came right up behind me on the last lap so I let him go past, I didn't want to get put in. He pushed Nigel wide and I sneaked on the inside of Nigel and was right behind Danny at the finish."

Circling the Belle Vue track alongside a top driver like Danny Wainman in only his first shale meeting proved that Hunter had natural talent behind the wheel. It was unlike anything he'd every raced before, but he'd found himself on the pace after only three races.

"I didn't think I'd got a good place, maybe tenth or something. When I went round the track again I saw Danny pulled up where the top three normally go and Nigel was behind him, so I thought I must have been a lap down. My dad thought I was third so he went up to the steward's box, and it turned out I was. So I had to go and get my first trophy from Nigel in the pits!"

Hunter raced the rest of his first month as a white top, benefiting from starting at the front of the grid with the other newer and slower drivers. The first regrading saw him with enough points to put him on the threshold of becoming a red top, but the sensible choice was made to promote him only to yellow, one grid slot further back than the whites.

"I had a really good month from yellow," Hunter recalls. "I got a few half-decent results. In the UK Open Championship meeting, I came second in the first heat. Then I had a good meeting at Birmingham, where I got two seconds and a first – my only race win. I had a few good results at Buxton too."

The learning process was far from over.

"I remember the first big hit I got. I got tangled up with Paul Carter and ended up going into the fence. I was shook up and thought, 'bloody hell, that was a massive hit!' But watching back on video, I was just tootling back into the fence – it was nothing!"

This was a driver who was used to racing in a kart with a thirty horsepower engine. Suddenly he was enclosed in a steel cab on top of an engine with twenty times the power. And don't forget the bumpers.

"The first two or three months were not the most pleasant thing. It was horrible getting hits when I didn't know what to do and I wasn't very fast. But within three or four months I got used to the contact. I like to think I could go into the fence fairly hard now and not bother about it too much."

Good results from yellow saw Hunter leapfrog blue and move to red in the next regrading. Suddenly, he found himself starting towards the back of the grid alongside some of the top names in the sport: John Lund, Paul Harrison, Dan Johnson.

"That was fine by me. I wanted to go from white, to yellow, to red. I didn't want to do blue because it's the worst place to start!"

What's perhaps more impressive is that Hunter maintained his red top for the rest of the season, never dipping particularly close to blue. He quietly and consistently picked up top ten placings.

"Race to race, it always changes," Hunter explains. "They are never the same. One meeting at Stoke I had a cracking start and got away from all the reds and got sixth in the final, but then at one Coventry meeting I got put in the fence by Josh Smith and never got back into it. I always get stuck in as much as I can and I want to be following the rest of the reds around."

It's fair to say that Hunter has rarely challenged for the chequered flag. He wasn't able to follow up his first race win with another, although he did pick up five second places over the season. Instead, it was his commitment that saw him securely hold onto his red roof. Attending forty meetings – the seventh-highest number of all drivers – meant that the consistent top ten finishes soon added up. Perhaps more importantly, it has allowed Hunter and his team to build up experience and learn the art of stock car racing.

"Throughout the year, we've learnt that aspect," Hunter agrees. "When we started, we didn't know how to set up a stock car at all. I get great personal support from my girlfriend Charlotte and advice from Peter Falding, but when it comes to setup and maintenance there's a core of three people. My dad sets up my car with me and the main mechanic is Arran, he does all the welding of the cars with me during the week. I've taken a stupid amount of damage this year. I seem to have been in the thick of everything and have damaged every part of the car that I could, so it's been a bit difficult."

Hunter also admits that he has had to learn the nuances of how to get the best out of each car and both surfaces.

"Tarmac racing is a lot closer. You have to be on it 99% of the time, to be hitting all of the apexes. It's quite straightforward really. You throttle, you turn left, you throttle again. Shale racing is more of an art. You've got to have your brakes right, you don't want to be stepping out too much, you don't want to be understeering outwards too much, you start playing on the throttle coming out, you're always sideways. It's two completely different things."

Yet Hunter wants to continue to improve.

Hunter tries a different wheel configuration – it wasn't really a success!

"I've not done as well as I want to, although I'm probably a bit harsh on myself. At the start of the season I said that if I got to blue and won Novice of the Year then that would do me. But now I'm looking at myself after some meetings thinking I'm not happy, I'm nowhere near where I want to be or fast enough. I'm just picking up points and places at the back but I want to be at the front and competing for nearly every race that I'm in."

He may not have been at the front of every race, but he certainly was at the front of the Novice of the Year championship. Indeed, he was so far ahead that he was out of sight, finishing light-years ahead of Karl Roberts.

The Novice of the Year championship offers a challenge to the newer drivers to the sport – those who, like Hunter, are building up experience but are yet to challenge for regular race wins or titles. It can be a springboard to great things. In one particularly strong period between 2005 and 2008, it was won by Tom Harris, Dan Johnson, Ryan Harrison and Danny Wainman. Yet since then, no Novice of the Year has progressed to major championship success or earned the flashing amber lights of superstar grade. Many have looked promising for a short period, only to disappear just as quickly as they emerged. The much-feted 'young guns' of the mid-noughties are starting to grow up and there hasn't been a new generation to replace them.

Can Will Hunter reverse the trend?

Smoking tyres – Hunter is increasingly confident going from red

"The thing that I've done differently," Hunter explains, "is that I've not come into the sport saying, 'I'm going to do this' and 'I'm going to do that' and treated everybody with disrespect. When the red tops were coming past and I was a white top, I let them past. I think that's been repaid now that I'm going from red. I think they know that I'm a good driver and I have the pace."

Success in the next few seasons certainly won't come as easily as the Novice of the Year title. Hunter knows that he isn't the finished article yet.

"I'm quite cautious and forward-seeing. If there's going to be a crash I'll miss it, where everybody else will go piling in. I like to think that as I go on my pace will be my strong point. I'll be fast probably. Precise. But there are going to be times next year when I'm building up my respect. I am going to have a few battles and a few hard hits with red tops because I think I need to at this stage. Once I get going and I'm on my own, my pace is spot on, but when I'm battling it needs to be a bit better."

It's time to move up a gear. After a promising first season, Hunter needs to convert the top ten finishes that have seen him comfortably win the Novice of the Year, into top three finishes that will see him compete for other honours.

"Most red tops will say the same – I want to win a few finals. Right now I'm a good driver, but I'm not a top driver like Dan Johnson, Tom Harris or Craig Finnikin. I'd like to be a top driver, winning a few finals or a major championship:

Kings of the Oval

Red sky at night, red tops' delight!

European, British or even World. I'll go all out and try to do it, but realistically I just want to become a top driver, one of the best."

Formula 1 can't afford to become a closed shop. New blood is needed to freshen things up, to challenge the status quo, to rattle a few back bumpers. Hopefully Will Hunter is the first of a new band of young drivers – Jordan Falding and Bradley Harrison are among those aiming to join him in 2015, perhaps Frankie Wainman Junior Junior too.

Move over young guns. The next generation is coming.

Like father, like son

It's in the blood – many drivers are following in their fathers' footsteps when they get behind the wheel of a Formula 1 stock car. Between them, Warren and Will Hunter have passed the chequered flag first eleven times, but they've got a little way to go yet if they want to compete with these great father and son pairings...

Stuart and Andy Smith, 1988 race wins: The most successful father-son double-act in the sport's first sixty years, their success is even more remarkable when you consider that both ended their racing careers when they were still at the top of the sport. Stuart's other son has also been pretty successful – between them, Stuart Senior and Stuart Junior have amassed 1733 race wins.

Frankie and Frankie Wainman, 1842 race wins: Frankie Senior won three consecutive silver roofs in the mid-eighties. That wasn't good enough for Frankie Junior – he won ten on the bounce between 1996 and 2005. There's also another son on the racetrack – Frankie Senior and Danny Wainman have a total of 797 race wins.

Willie and Paul Harrison, 924 race wins: The only father and son that can claim lineage from the present to the beginnings of the sport in 1954, the Harrisons are

a popular fixture on the racetrack and in the bar. Never ones to rush into anything, Willie won his World Championship title after 29 years in the sport. Paul was relatively quick – he only took 27!

Bert and Craig Finnikin, 595 race wins: Bert currently totals the seventh-highest number of race wins and a career grand slam of major titles. Craig looks set to rival his achievements, having already won three of the major championships.

Rod and Peter Falding, 588 race wins: For 25 years, Rod Falding was a solid driver, picking up a handful of wins each season. He'll be the first to admit that his achievements were quickly overshadowed when his son came on the scene. Peter became the youngest World Champion in 1986 and added a further three World Final wins through the rest of his career.

Doug and Alan Wardropper, 516 race wins: The original father-son stock car partnership, the Wardroppers were active during the fifties and sixties. Only Dad won the World Championship, but both picked up the National Points and British titles. Considering that they only raced for a total of 23 years, their combined number of race wins is superb.

BRITISH CHAMPION

2

PAUL HARRISON

Prepare the car. Prepare the driver. Win the race.

It sounds easy, but it's not quite that simple in practice. When the first major championship race of the 2014 season came round, Paul Harrison was possibly as ill-prepared as he ever had been. Both he and his car were still struggling to come to terms with an incident six months before.

"We probably need to go back to the end of the 2013 season," Harrison explains. "I had a smash at the Skegness Shootout round, a real bad crash. It was a wet, greasy track and I was doing really well, Tom Harris caught me up and came past but I hung onto him. Carl Pickering was winning. As we went into the last lap, Pickering messed up going down the back straight and it looked like I was going to get an easy second place. But as I went up the inside of a white top, he saw Pickering turn the wrong way and panicked. The white top did a big left turn. I knew that it wasn't good. He washed my front end into the inner tyre wall and I dug in and bent the steering wheel. It spat me back out into the traffic and Paul Hines hit my back inside, flat out towards the end of the straight. It spun me, 180 degrees, as Lee Fairhurst hit my outside front and spun me back again. That effectively wrecked my tarmac car. It was a complete mess. The chassis was bent dramatically at the front and back. The cab had gone over. It was an utter mess. My arm came out of the cab and bent backwards and it was the first time that I had been unconscious in a stock car. When I came round, I didn't feel good. It was a real bad one. Nothing was broken, but in the World Final a month or so before,

I had a real bad head-on impact through a cloud of dust with a Dutch driver and broke my sternum, so I upset that again."

An injured car and an injured body: Harrison was forced to ask himself some tough questions. Was it worthwhile spending money to fix his car, only to go back out and potentially do more damage to himself?

"It's the twilight years of my career, I know that, but I didn't feel that it was the end. It would have been easy to say that's it, I'm going to pack it in, but I didn't want to end on a whimper. If I'm going to retire, I want to retire on my terms. So I spoke to Tom Harris about putting my car right. We could have straightened it on a commercial jig but the cost was high. I wasn't going to gain anything doing that so I took the decision to have a new car."

Over the winter, Tom Harris was kept busy in his garage while Harrison recuperated. Six months after the enforced end to his tarmac season at Skegness, it was time to start again on the hard stuff.

"The first time I saw the new car was the Birmingham and Hednesford double-header," Harrison remembers. "We had problems with it at Birmingham and sorted it out for Hednesford the next day. It's not one of my favourite tracks, but I still got the fastest time of the meeting. The car was fast and I got good results all day, I was really pleased with it. The next thing was the Good Friday meeting at Skegness and I got stuck in the fence double-hard by Ryan Harrison. The car was a mess again. I sent it off to Tom to put right because I'd been so happy with it, I told him to bring it back just as it was. I got the car back and had to get used to it again for the British Championship at Birmingham."

The car was on fire at Hednesford, but there was no guarantee that it would be back to normal after the damage sustained at Skegness. Luckily, Tom Harris had managed to work his magic in the workshop. In the practice session before the meeting, Harrison set the second-quickest time. The car was ready. But what about the driver? Harrison had suffered plenty himself, and fixing that wasn't as easy.

"The injuries that I sustained at the back end of 2013 pretty much stayed in my mind for the season," Harrison reveals. "I got in the car with a different mind frame to how I normally did. I felt noticeably different about myself and getting injured, often backing out of a situation. But I still took a few knocks and bangs, something that I've not had in thirty years. I was hurt again when Ryan Harrison stuck me off the end of the straight in my new car. Then at a meeting final at Sheffield, Josh Smith was leading and I caught him up. John Lund was doing a slow lap round the inside, half on the track, half on the kerb. I had to go up the inside of Josh but outside of John. On the exit it put me a bit wider than I'd like. Paul Hines took the opportunity to barge up my inside when I was a bit vulnerable and sent me towards the fence. As it does at Sheffield, the front bumper dug into a post

and spat me back out into the track in front of a fast-charging Mark Gilbank who hit my back outside wheel and sent me on a full rotation. I sat in the car on the infield for the rest of the race trying to get my breath back and managed to get the car pushed off to the back of the bus. I got out of the car and curled up on the bus in agony. I was conscious that I was putting my body on the line."

Harrison was approaching racing with a different attitude. Never one of the most aggressive drivers, he might previously have backed out of a dangerous situation in order to protect his car. But he had never backed out of something in order to protect himself. For the first time he felt vulnerable, and that made him cautious.

"I'd started getting on track and feeling like I was making numbers up a little bit. Then, before the British Championship meeting, Andrew Smith said to me, 'what are you messing at? You've told me how good your car is, you've told me it's the best thing you've ever driven on tarmac – so why are you driving it like a tosser? I know you can drive, you know you can drive. Go out there and show us what you can do!' It got in my head."

With Smith's words ringing in his ears, Harrison determined to make the most of his opportunity. As promised, he wasn't going to go out on a whimper.

"I won the first heat and won my next heat and I could tell that things were good. I knew after getting two first places that I would be somewhere near the

2014 British Championship grid – Harrison was first at the start, first at the finish

front of a field packed with top names. There might be life in the old dog yet. In my last heat, while I was on track with dry tyres on, it started drizzling. Mick Sworder and Frankie Wainman Junior were quicker than me. The car had a little bit of understeer, which in the first two heats was helping me round the corners in the second half of the race – Birmingham has a tendency to go loose – but in the wet the understeer was exaggerated and it pushed on and got worse as the race went on. Suddenly I'd lost the edge that I thought I had in the first two heats. In the last heat, which I wasn't in, it started to rain heavily and the drivers geared up accordingly. I watched Stuart Smith Junior and he was blisteringly fast. He had rally tyres on the front and he looked like he was racing on dry tarmac. I thought there was no way that I would be able to match that sort of pace in the wet."

When the grid was put together, Harrison's two firsts and a fourth were good enough for pole position. The two drivers with the next best results, on the outside of the front row and inside of the second row, were yellow tops Rob Cowley and John Dowson. Frankie Wainman Junior was on the outside of the second row and Stuart Smith Junior was on the inside of the third.

"The track was still wet," Harrison recalls. "I needed to think outside the box. I'd never raced with rally tyres on both front wheels on tarmac, but I saw that Stuart had done that. We put them on and had to make some adjustments to the shockers and went to weigh the car on the scales, but they weren't working right. We'd just guessed at it and didn't know if it was legal, we had to hope for the best."

Out on track, Harrison began to think about his strategy for the race.

"The first bend was going to be essential. I needed to get away. Frankie would be going hell for leather, so would Stuart, they saw how quick I was and would be having a shot to try and stop me getting away. I thought that Rob Cowley and John Dowson could be a cushion, but they could also be like bullets out of a gun and Stuart and Frankie were going to try and use them to shoot me."

As often happens in stock car racing, the plans were thrown out of the window as soon as the green flag fell.

"In an ideal world I would have been in a straight line off the corner before I pressed go and the others, particularly Stuart, might still have a bit of left turn left to do before they got in a straight line. But before we got to where I was ready to go, Cowley had booted it. I could see that he had gone slightly sideways. My focus was nailing it without drifting the back end, getting as much drive as I could get. I picked up and went down the straight. I didn't even look in my mirror, I turned into the corner as tight as I could and the front end bit like I was on rails. It turned better in the wet with the rally tyre on than it did in the dry with my normal tarmac tyre on. When I spat out of the bend, I'd already pulled a decent gap. Dowson was behind me and I didn't have a clue about the rest."

That first corner effectively won the British Championship. Smith and Wainman didn't get close, tripping over each other and Cowley as they went under the starter. The only clean starters were Harrison and Dowson, and Harrison soon pulled away.

"I had to make fast laps as quick as I could while I had a clear track, but I don't think I managed to complete two laps before I was catching others up. I wanted to get past the backmarkers as quickly as possible to put them between me and the others chasing in case there was a yellow flag. Every single lap I was concentrating on driving as fast as I could. A quick glance in the mirror showed that nobody was catching me, but in conditions like that, you can't see everything and somebody might suddenly appear. I got my head down and kept blasting away. The spray was clearing so the track was drying and I didn't know whether the rally tyres would lose their edge. I started catching up red tops, good drivers who were in their own fight. I couldn't afford to get mixed up their battles. It was a case of catching them up, giving them a little tap so they knew I was there, and hoping they would give me a yard because I was so much quicker. I remember catching John Lund and Paul Hines, then I was in with the likes of Rob Speak and Lee Fairhurst – bloody good drivers!"

Of all the championship races in the 2014, Harrison's victory in the British was the most convincing and comprehensive. Even if Stuart Smith Junior had managed to start well, it's likely that Harrison would have had enough speed to win. He was in the fastest car and drove a clean race. Yet the best car and the best driver don't always win – this is stock cars, after all.

"With about five to go I could see that I was catching Scott Davids," Harrison remembers. "Sometimes he can be a little bit erratic. It doesn't matter whether you're leading or whether you're five laps in front, if he's concentrating on his own race and you get in his way, he doesn't care what happens to you. He'd put you on a car in front if it would gain him a place. I could do with not passing Scott but I didn't know what was going on behind. I gave him a little one to pass him but didn't seem to be shaking him off as quickly as I hoped. It looked like he was going to come in and he got bigger in my mirror but then he backed off. I was away."

Harrison passed the black-and-white chequered flag to win, allowing him to wear the black-and-white chequered roof signifying the British Champion for the next twelve months.

"I was so elated when I went past the flag. I pulled up, leapt out of the car and onto the rostrum. Craig Finnikin said to me that he was still racing and as he went past he could see me already stood up there on the podium! I was absolutely overjoyed. Then after the presentations I remembered that the car had to go to the scales. It seemed like we were waiting ages at the back of the bus – I didn't go with the car because the pressure was doing my head in. I was feeling uneasy. But the scales still weren't working so I was confirmed as the winner. The first thing we did when we got the car back home was put the car on the scales and it was comfortably in tolerance. We were dead chuffed – we knew that we had the setup for a wet track."

In the nick of time, car and driver came together. Prepared car plus prepared driver equals race win!

"The decision to have the new car, which was a little bit extravagant considering the stage of my career, was totally justified. It was the right decision."

Harrison makes no attempt to hide the fact that his racing career is winding down. It's been a long journey. His time behind the wheel started in 1977, in Ministox, at just eight years old. The lower age limit for Ministox was actually ten, but Paul's dad pushed him towards it. "Can he drive?" the promoter asked. "Of course he can, I taught him!" his father answered. There were few better teachers than Willie Harrison.

Paul graduated from Ministox and made his Formula 1 debut as a fresh-faced sixteen year old at the end of the 1985 season. Marty McFly was about to go *Back to the Future* and Jennifer Rush's 'Power of Love' was the number one single. Stuart Smith was the World Champion, Frankie Wainman held the National Points title, Bert Finnikin and Danny Clarke were the British and European Champions. His

As quick to get to the podium as he is round the track!

dad was stock car racing's Father of the House, in his third decade of racing, the only survivor from the debut season of 1954.

Father and son raced alongside each other for five years until Willie finally hung up his helmet, 37 years after first picking it up, allowing Paul to inherit his famous number 2. It wasn't possible to compare their achievements yet; they were at opposite ends of their careers. Instead, Paul was often compared with another second-generation driver who had joined the grid with high expectations. Frankie Wainman Junior started a couple of years after Harrison but, on 1 May 1988, both drivers rolled out on track under a red roof having achieved star grade for the first time. But which of the bright young things would win the first title?

It was Harrison. The 1991 British Championship was held at a wet Buxton Raceway. Harrison, in a new tarmac car, made a good start and led from the green flag to the chequered. Sound familiar? The circumstances were pretty similar to Harrison's 2014 victory, give or take a couple of decades!

"I did the work in the heats, got the pole and led from flag to flag with Ray Tyldesley a comfortable distance in my mirror. I'd finished second to John Lund the previous year and built a car for the new season. It was the third car that I'd built. It was similar to John Lund's tarmac car of the time. I shamelessly copied it really! It had single-leaf rear suspension with air shockers, the other two cars I'd built were multi-leafed springs."

Making a start under number 22

Harrison lost his title the following year to none other than his young rival, Frankie Wainman Junior, who won his first major title on the Coventry shale. Then, in 1993, Harrison reclaimed it.

"1993 was another wet British Championship meeting at Long Eaton," Harrison remembers. "I did reasonable in my heats and started the final on the outside of row three. I made a good start and came out of the turn in second place behind Peter Falding. I was chasing him down, but he was very much the man at that time and I knew that he took no prisoners in terms of driving style. But I was catching him. If I went past him, there was only one place that he was going to put me – on a fence post. I went down the back straight into the turn and I thought, right, he's going to get a big one. Peter started to pull over at the point where I was committed. Another time, would I have gone up his inside, who knows? But he'd pulled over and I'd committed and I dropped him straight on a fence post. He stopped dead, game over. Off I went. There was a fast-charging Bert Finnikin but I managed to maintain a gap. As I got to a few laps to go I heard a rattle. All the pressures seemed OK so I kept going, somewhat anxiously to the flag."

It was a second British Championship title, and still only 24 years old. Moreover, Harrison had stopped Peter Falding – one of the top drivers of the day, and Harrison's best friend – from winning his maiden British crown.

"I went into the bar afterwards and I could see Peter. I approached the bar expecting that he might have something to say to me. At the top of the steps he stood in my way and held out his hand. He said, 'I was just pulling out of the way, if you hadn't done that to me I'd have done it to you at the end of the next straight!'"

For the next nineteen years, Harrison never finished lower than sixth in the season-long grading chart. He was consistently fast and always a challenger, but it was a period largely starved of championship success. One UK Open and two European titles were relatively slim pickings for such a top driver. Over the same period, Wainman won 24 major championships, not including those he picked up abroad.

It seemed that Harrison was going to go down in history as a driver who peaked relatively early in his career, always the bridesmaid, the best driver never to win the World Championship. That all changed in 2011, his career season. It started, once again, with victory at the British Championship.

"The one I won at King's Lynn in 2011 stands out in my mind as being one of my best races," Harrison says. "I did well in the heats and got pole position but they wet the track more than I would have liked and I got spun and turned around completely on the first corner. The gaggle of cars picked me up and pointed me in the right direction. I'd stalled so got in gear and restarted. I think I'd dropped to thirteenth but at least the car was in one piece. I did another lap and got slammed round the back of Tim Warwick's stranded car. The yellows came out for him and I got back to the top ten. It wasn't over. In no time I'd fought my way to third and just as I managed to pass Dan Johnson there were yellows again. On the restart Dan managed to get the better of me and forced me out wide. Stuart Smith Junior managed to get away and was more than a full straight in front. I thought the race was over. But I got my head down and reeled him in, and with five or six to go I thought I might catch him. I gave him a good one at the start of the last lap which sent him up the wall and delayed him enough for me to come out of the bend feeling confident enough that I'd done enough, only to go into the final corner to see Stuart in my mirror coming at me – he was going to give it everything he'd got. I gave a little press in the middle of the corner and that just got me away from him."

It's a race that Harrison considered to be one of his best, not just for the nature of the victory – starting at the front, being relegated back and seemingly out of contention, clawing his way back to the front and winning on the last lap – but for the context of the race.

"When I won the British the first couple of times, you just got to write British Champion on your car. It was only in later years that you got the black-and-white chequered roof. Having raced under a red roof since the late eighties, it was something special. I remember being interviewed afterwards and saying that I truly believed that the best was yet to come. And how right I was!"

Harrison followed up his British Championship victory by winning his World Championship Semi-Final at Skegness, giving him a front row start in the World Final. He was a veteran of the prestigious race – it was his 23rd appearance – yet he had never won it. Three second-placed finishes looked like they were going to be as good as it got.

Part of the trouble was the immense pressure that Harrison put on himself. He made no secret of the fact that the World Championship was the one that he wanted to win. He geared up his entire season around it. Yet that pressure was having a negative effect. Sleepless nights leading up to the World Final were not the best preparation. Being tense and tight in the big race did not allow him to perform at his best.

Harrison is a popular figure in the pits, always ready to crack a joke and flash his cheeky smile. Yet his extrovert nature hides the fact that he is an intelligent, inward-looking character. He is very self-critical and analytical of his own actions and failings. Sometimes he can be his own worst enemy, talking himself out of the race before it has even started.

What Harrison needed was the input of somebody who could break through the barriers that he was imposing on himself. That man was Mike Finnegan, a psychologist who had worked with some of the top names in sport, including Darren Clarke, Andrew Flintoff and David Moyes. All it took was thirty minutes on the phone the evening before the World Final.

Harrison woke the next morning a different man. He was in the zone, determined, ruthlessly upbeat. Nobody was going to stop him winning the gold roof. In one of the best World Final races of recent years, he manoeuvred through the first few laps, never outside the top four, before pouncing on Dan Johnson to take the lead at half-distance. At long last, he won the title he wanted the most. It had taken him 27 years to do it. It had taken his father 29 – the Harrisons don't like to rush things!

Everything looked like it was falling into place again three years later. After winning his fourth British title at Birmingham, Harrison went to the World Semi-Final at Skegness and came away with victory.

"I was on the outside of the second row in the semi-final, which is not my preferred position because you just don't know what is going to happen. At Skegness, a lot of it can be about the first bend and I was acutely aware of that. It was all about the start. I always feel that if I can get a good start, I stand a good chance at the latter stages of the races. But there's a lot that can happen at the start that you can't account for, other drivers, you don't know what's going to happen."

"I had Mick Sworder behind me who was potentially going to go in with a big hit. Stuart Smith Junior was a couple of rows behind, and Mark Gilbank, both big hitters too. I looked around and on the inside of the second and third rows were Paul Hines and Craig Finnikin. If I was going to cut in anywhere, I was going to cut in front one of them, but they're good drivers, nobody is going to let you in, they all want to maintain their position. Ideally, if you're on the inside, you're going to go into the corner on the bumper of the car in front and those on the outside are going to be hung out to dry. You're lucky if you don't get driven up the fence. But Craig Finnikin had a brand new tyre on his outside rear. Now my experience is that the very first time you use a brand new tyre on tarmac, it can be a little bit loose and cause oversteer. Potentially, when he booted it to go, Craig might break traction a little and I may be able to let Hines go and dive in immediately behind him."

And you thought they just booted the accelerator and aimed at the car in front! No, it's a little more subtle than that.

"As we're going round the rolling lap, I was leaving a bit of a gap to Rob Speak in front. I'd convinced myself that I was going to get inbetween Finnikin and Hines. At the point where we were just about ready to go, Sworder was running up my backside and I thought sod it, just go. Just as I was changing into second, I heard Paul Hines miss his gear. The perfect gap opened up and I was straight in front of him and accelerating up the inside of Speak. A blistering start! We got to the starter and I could see Speaky hanging out wide. There was only one thing on his mind in hanging out as wide as that and that's to have a shot at Tom Harris in pole position. Somebody nudged my back bumper and that helped me round the corner and into the lead down the back straight. Tom was out wide and I couldn't tell whether he'd hit the fence or not, but I could see Speak and I could tell that he was still hungry, so I thought I'd stay on his inside round the corner. As I went in, Paul Hines nibbled my back bumper and set me up for the corner again. I had a good straight past the starter into the first bend for the second time. No nudge. Come on, this is it! I did a couple of good laps and the yellows came out so I had it all to do again. The green flag fell; I had another good start and got away. A few laps and the yellows came out again. I would have to win this one a few times over. We set off again, another good one, but Rob made a better contact with Paul which touched my back bumper. But I was away again. That was it. Fast laps, nice and tidy, every one to make it count. I pulled out a gap and won by a fair distance."

Both the British Championship and World Semi-Final were won with great first laps. The stars seemed to be aligning again. First the British, then the Semi-Final – could Harrison repeat his hat-trick of 2011 and win the gold roof again?

"It didn't bode well right from the start," Harrison explains. "When we went out on the parade lap, the pace car was too slow and Lee, my mechanic who was driving the car, stalled. He tried to restart and the starter button, which is pressed hundreds of times throughout the season, decided to pack in there and then. One of the worst things that can happen in a stock car is not having the ability to start your car to get out of trouble. I was out of sorts already."

The mental preparation that Harrison needed wasn't there this time. He wasn't in the right headspace.

"I set up my car for the second half of the race and never got into it as a result. I just needed three laps to settle in and I'd have been ok. I have understeer on shale in the first few laps which was letting them get the shots on me and making it worse. The yellows came out and I had dropped a few. The car still wasn't right at that stage. It happened again on the next restart, I got gobbled up, then it went pear-shaped, I ended up getting collected and spun out and the car stalled. Game over."

Now that he has won the World Championship and had his year under the gold roof, Harrison admits that failing in the World Final is not as disappointing as it used to be. He can afford to be a little more philosophical.

"I know I'm coming towards the end of my career. If it is going to be my last season, I don't want to go out and make the numbers up. I've got two great cars; I want to make it a good season. If I'm going to go in half-heartedly, I might as well pack in now. I want to pack in with some credibility."

There are occasional reminders that Harrison is in the twilight years of his career. He pauses and wonders whether he was the oldest World Finalist in 2014. With a laugh, he realises that John Lund, Graeme Barr and Mal Brown were older.

"It's a bugger when you're struggling to think of drivers on the grid who are older than you!" Harrison jokes. "I don't see myself as old and I don't feel old, but it's a fact of life. When I watch the Under 25 Championship, most of the drivers weren't born by the time that I was a superstar. These kids are coming through and there are some fantastic drivers among them. To see my son, Bradley, coming through with them makes me more accepting of my own situation. Watching him will give me something extra. The likes of Dave Johnson tell me that it's brilliant to watch your son racing and doing well, even better than when you race yourself, so I'm looking forward to that."

Long gone are the days when Paul Harrison was the youngest driver on the grid. Over three decades, he has traded bumper paint with some legends from the history of the sport. Who does he think is the best he has raced against?

"You can't ask me that! It's like asking me to choose my favourite child! I raced against Stuart Senior, Dave Mellor, Bert Finnikin, Nigel Whorton, Chris Elwell, Len Wolfenden, Frankie Wainman Senior, Bobby Burns. I've raced against them

Tied in third place for the most British titles

all. And the modern day greats: Frankie Wainman Junior, Andy Smith and Stuart Smith Junior. People say that the golden era of the sport has gone, but there are some bloody good drivers behind the wheel today too. Tom Harris, Lee Fairhurst, Dan Johnson. It's a tough one that. I can't answer!"

Three decades on and winding down his racing career, Paul Harrison should feel assured of his own place in stock car history. Four British Championships – a feat he shares with Andy Smith, only John Lund and Frankie Wainman Junior have won it more – is a magnificent achievement. Yet Harrison's biggest achievement is probably that he will be remembered as one of the most popular and likeable characters that the sport has ever known. Sometimes that counts for more than silverware.

Harrison's big hitters

In thirty years in stock cars, Paul Harrison has had the pleasure – or should that be pain – of racing against some of stock car racing's biggest hitters. Here is a selection of the hard nuts...

Bobby Burns: "Bobby was just a hard case and he raced his stock car that way too. He didn't take any crap on or off the track; mess with him at your peril. Having said that, out of the car he wasn't angry or anything, he had a cheerful humorous manner, you could just tell he was hard!"

Kev Smith: "Kev came into the job to have fun; he deliberately went out of his way to use the bumper. This caused other drivers to race against Kev differently, you couldn't pass him without getting a good hiding so you had to be clever with him, make sure he couldn't get on you next bend. This meant dropping another car on him or putting him away because if you didn't and he got a sniff you were getting it, even if you had passed him clean. I think he became his own worst enemy because he became disillusioned with the racing, but it was the result of drivers racing differently against him."

Frankie Wainman Junior: "Mr Stock Car, fanatical about our sport and fantastic with it. He came into our sport wanting to be the best, prepared to do whatever it takes to achieve it. That meant taking no prisoners, ever. To be number one you have to be like that, to take on all challengers and never give in. Very few have got the better of Frankie and to be like that, consistently, for nearly thirty years, has meant knowing how and when to use the bumper. If you gave it him you were getting it back. You could argue that he didn't like it back, but let's be honest, who does? Still to this day, Frankie doesn't like being passed and has to wallop you when you pass him."

Peter Falding: "Up until winning the 1986 World Final, I don't remember Peter being particularly aggressive, but having done so in only his fourth season of racing and at such a young age, I guess there were plenty who wanted to have a nibble at him. Peter obviously didn't like being nibbled and adopted an aggressive driving style, not discriminating against any grade. This led to legendary battles with Frankie Senior and John Lund. He was lured to the bright lights of circuit racing and returned to win two more World Finals when he wasn't really trying. His track craft won him those, he had a stock car brain, he knew how to build and set up stock cars and he knew how to use the bumper. If he wasn't the fastest in a race he could still win it with the bumper – you can't do that in circuit racing!"

The Smiths: "It was the last meeting at the old Belle Vue and Stuart Smith's last ever competitive meeting: I was leading the final on a damp, greasy track and the lap boards were out. I could see a car catching in the mirror but couldn't make out who it was. But I didn't have long to think about it because as soon as Stuart got a sniff of my back bumper he dropped me on a parked car in the fence to win his 500th final! Both Andrew and Stuart Junior inherited their dad's use of the front bumper. Andrew is a perfectionist and master of his craft. His use of the front bumper was sublime and he feared no one, quite prepared to mix it with anyone until he felt the score was settled... in his favour! A brilliant stock car driver. Stuart Junior came into the job with high expectations. Not only did he win the World and British Championships early in his career, he went on to win the first National Series Shootout with brutal, no-nonsense bumper work which remains one of his trademarks."

Mick Sworder: "There had been talk and speculation for years that Mick might progress to F1 but it didn't happen until 2011, by which time he was a veteran of the ovals. I think he realised he should have made the switch years before. No doubt a very talented and very entertaining driver, I feel that he sometimes uses the front bumper out of sheer frustration at his late entry into F1, resulting in spectacular fencings for the recipient. I have been on the receiving end of his bumper twice, both at Coventry, and both times leaving me parked and narked!"

Phil Haigh: "A low-grade budget-racing entertainer who said that stock car racing is like snooker, you have to pot the reds first! In an attempt to raise sponsorship he once charged a £1 to anyone who wanted to write their name on his car with a black marker pen – I remember Peter Falding giving him a fiver to keep him sweet, but I don't know whether it was a fiver well spent or not! He was a crowd pleaser, a trier, and a pain in the arse if you were a red top!"

Len Wolfenden: "I raced against Len during a few appearances he made at the end of his career and I knew to stay out of his way! He was the bane of Stuart Smith's life for a few years and took great pleasure in tormenting him. In the 1984 World Final, I recall him waiting for Stuart and driving in front of him with his brakes on to spoil his race. Stuart still won, but when I once asked him who had been his hardest rival, he had no hesitation in citing Len."

Rob Speak: "His records in both F2 and F1 speak for themselves. Rob just loves racing and using the front bumper comes naturally to him. Rob is clever with his bumper and uses it not just to entertain but to win – he will pass a car clean if he thinks it's the quickest way forward but then unleash the front bumper to devastating effect when he chooses."

SCOTTISH & UNDER 25 CHAMPION

84

TOM HARRIS

Winning the Formula 1 stock car World Championship brings with it the right to race under a gold roof until the next World Championship. It's an honour that every driver in the sport strives to attain, yet racing with the gold roof is not necessarily all it's made out to be. Some drivers crumble under the pressure. Perhaps unused to starting every race at the back with the superstars, they struggle to win races. Some put extra pressure on themselves, feeling the need to show off the gold roof to the best of their ability, to prove that the World Final win wasn't a fluke.

Others take to it like a duck to water. Winning the gold roof can ease the pressure they put on themselves, allowing them to relax. They no longer have anything to prove. Tom Harris certainly fits into the latter category. He won 28 races under the gold roof, a figure bettered only by Andy Smith, Frankie Wainman Junior and John Lund over the past twenty years.

Harris won the 2013 World Final at King's Lynn. Starting from the outside of the second row, he survived a first-lap battle with defending champion Lee Fairhurst and quickly pulled in early leader Ryan Harrison, whose deep line into the corners was not as fast as Harris' tighter turns. On the fifth lap, Harris drove up the inside without touching his opponent to take the lead.

"The car was horrendous in the first few laps," Harris reveals. "When I moved the brakes to the rear, there was no looking back. I managed to pass Ryan and get a gap. I didn't realise how far in front I was. The car didn't feel particularly fast but

Winning the World Final in 2013...

we looked at the lap times afterwards and I was about three-tenths of a second quicker than everybody else."

Not all World Finals are classics. Harris was fortunate that he was pretty much untested on his way to victory – good for him, less so for the spectators. However, even an easy World Final win is still a big deal when you're the one behind the wheel.

"I wouldn't say it was easy! It was a daunting race. You're leading the World Championship. Cars are crashing all over the place. The halfway flag comes out and then you're waiting for the five lap boards. You've backed off a bit but you don't want to back off too much. You're watching what's going on. You don't want to hammer the car too much because you don't want a mechanical failure. I found a gap with Ben Hurdman in front and Will Yarrow behind. I didn't want to catch Ben but I didn't want Will to catch me, I just wanted to sit there. I could see on the scoreboard that Ryan was second and I wasn't too fazed because I knew that I was quicker than him on a slick track. But when Craig Finnikin got into second I started to worry about where he was – I knew that Craig was quick on a slick track."

At the start of that season, Harris had introduced a new shale car. He had one intention and one aim – to win the World Final.

...and wearing the gold roof en route to winning the Scottish Championship

"Everybody took the piss out of it," Harris says, "but every meeting we went to, we tried something different and started to put it all together. I built it to win the World Final. I was putting pressure on myself. I knew I was going to win the World Final; it was a matter of when, not if, it was going to happen."

With the World Championship trophy in his cabinet, Harris started the 2014 season with another new car. This time, however, he wasn't relying on it in a chase for new silverware.

"I built a new tarmac car and, when I got that on the pace, I was really enjoying the racing and everything was going well. Obviously I wanted to win, I race every week to win, but I enjoyed it a lot more. I didn't have as much pressure on my shoulders. I didn't have anything else to prove."

At the end of June, the F1 stock car travelling circus packed its bags and headed north of the border. It was the first time for five years that Scotland had hosted oval racing's premier formula. It was unknown territory for Harris, but he took to it better than anybody.

"It was the first time I'd been to Cowdenbeath. Everybody says that it's a man's track. There's not a lot of room but it's really fast. The corners are banked and there are four distinct corners. It's hard to pass because you hit someone wide and they end up where you want to be. It was quite a technical track. But I went out for practice in the afternoon and I broke the lap record three times! I was bouncing off

The training ground of oval motorsport – Harris in Ministox

the wall in the middle of the corner. When I came in, everybody was around the car. We had accusations that we were using tyre softener, so we got them to check everything out and go through the truck."

It wasn't the first time that Harris had suspicious looks cast in his direction. Nor would it be the last.

"They checked all the tyres we had and there were no problems. I was adamant that I was going to win the final, because when people do that it just makes you more determined to win. It was a hard race – a few big hits. Paul Ford got put in hard; then Rob Speak put me in. It hurt me, it winded me, but it didn't damage the car. I sat behind him and bided my time, waiting for him to make a mistake. I hit him wide and got past and by the end I'd pulled a straight on him again, away from a last bender."

Not only had Harris won the meeting final, with it came with the Scottish Championship title. He also picked up the meeting final the following day, at Lochgelly. Without doubt, the star of the Scottish weekend was Tom Harris. Two weeks later, he picked up his second championship title of the season. This time, it was the battle of the young guns: the Under 25 Championship.

"The Under 25 is a hard race," Harris reveals. "The year before, Lee Fairhurst won it when he was World and British Champion, I was the current National

Points Champion and Ryan Harrison was European Champion – all the major championships were held by under 25s."

The 2014 edition was on the Skegness tarmac and Harris' car was still flying after the Scottish weekend.

"It was a graded start – sometimes they go your way, sometimes they don't. I started dead last. I got up to second and I was in striking distance of Lee Fairhurst when he got a flat outside rear. Danny Wainman was behind me and he could see that Lee had a flat tyre and that it was going to be his only chance so he gave me a massive hit, but he half took himself out and then I just cruised."

Championship success eluded Harris for the rest of the season, but he remains happy with his haul. His Scottish crown and second Under 25 title have been added to his racing CV, one which has seen quite a few additions over the last four years.

Harris' path to stock car success started on two wheels rather than four. His father, Mick Harris, raced bangers and Formula 2 stock cars, but young Tom raced Motocross. Then, aged eight, Tom was knocked over by a car and suffered a broken leg. The same year, Mick made his debut in Formula 1 stock cars. By the time Tom recovered, two wheels didn't seem enough any more.

"I wanted a Ministox, so I raced them from when I was ten to fifteen. Then I had twelve months off because Dad had an old stock car chassis in the shed, one that Kev Smith had built, so I rebuilt that to use myself the following year. Then it was straight into Formula 1!"

When the green flag waved to start the first race of the 2005 season at King's Lynn, Harris was at the back as a novice driver. When the chequered flag waved to end the race, he was still at the back – the last finisher – but ninth place was still enough to qualify for the meeting final.

"It was completely unexpected to qualify for the final in my first ever race," Harris admits. "Although it was when I got onto tarmac that I started to win and it went on from there."

Once Harris shifted to starting from the front of the grid with the other white tops, he became uncatchable. Seven race wins over five meetings in April saw him shoot up the grading points chart.

"Because you could only go up two grades, I went from white to blue even though I was sixth in the National Points. I didn't score many points the following month from blue, but I still had enough points from the first month to go to red at the second regrading. The first time I raced from red at Coventry I didn't pass a car and still ended up seventh, it was quite surprising how different it was. I swopped between red and blue, red and blue for ages."

It was during his first demotion to blue top that Harris nearly pulled off a remarkable achievement. The British Championship, at Sheffield, saw him come close to winning a major championship in his debut season. Harris finished his three heats in third, fifth and first, good enough to earn him the outside of the front row for the championship race; Stuart Smith Junior was the only driver who did better. Harris had out-qualified Frankie Wainman Junior, Andy Smith and John Lund among others.

"It was the first time I started on the front row in a championship – quite daunting! Only Stuart and I made it through the first corner, everybody else went through the fence! I dropped back a couple of places, Frankie Wainman Junior and Mark Gilbank passed me, but I was really impressed with myself to get fourth."

Harris did win a title in his first season – Novice of the Year – and his father began to wind down his racing career as Tom became more competent and confident behind the wheel. Harris continued to leapfrog between red and blue grades until, at the age of 21, he committed himself to the sport in a full-time capacity.

"I always wanted to build stock cars. I always wanted to work for myself. But I didn't realise I'd end up working for myself building stock cars! When I was fifteen I rebuilt that car of my dad's so I could race it, but it really started when Gary Maynard bought a car and brought it here so I could revamp it."

Harris had previously completed an apprenticeship as a panel beater in Banbury and had a stint as a lorry driver in Preston, but on returning to the family home in Oxfordshire, he thought he could make a living in motorsport.

"I was winning on tarmac. Paul Harrison wanted to go faster so he brought his car here and I revamped that: engine mountings and axles, this and that. After a few of those, I decided to stop making other people's cars go faster. If you want a car you can have one, but you've got to have one of mine. There's plenty to keep me going!"

Building and maintaining his and other peoples' cars full-time gave Harris an extra insight and edge on the track, but he was also improving his racing technique too.

"You keep improving all the time. I try to improve myself as much as I do the cars," Harris says. "You've got to be smooth. Anybody can go around the track fast, anybody can do one lap fast, but you've got to do twenty laps fast, consistently smooth, in traffic as well. It's about finesse, hitting people at the right time so you don't slow down, being able to move two or three cars in a corner. It's natural to me now."

And it's not just about learning to use the front bumper. The back bumper is a vital part of a stock car too.

"It's also about taking hits," Harris agrees. "If I know that I'm going into the fence, I'm on the brakes, on the throttle, bouncing off the fence, and I still know where I'm going to be coming out of the corner. Rob Speak was hammering me once at Skegness. He put me in the fence hard. I bounced out, caught him up,

April 2005 – one of seven race wins under the white roof

tapped him, passed him and left him. I think that hurt him more than if I'd buried him."

Harris finished the 2011 season as the highest points scorer in the grading list – an achievement which didn't win him anything, but signalled his status as one of the top drivers in the formula. 2012 began with many predicting that Harris would now pop the champagne cork on top of the podium in a major championship. The first opportunity came at the British Championship in July. First and second place in Harris' two heats saw him start on pole position and he duelled with Craig Finnikin for the lead, but an early puncture put him out of the running.

"I never seemed to have any luck," Harris says. "I was getting a bit fed up of it."

The weekend after, the European Championship was another chance to get on the podium. Success! From dead last on the grid to first place by the end, Harris won his first major championship in brilliant style. Caught up in a crash which saw him lose four places, Harris came back through to move Dan Johnson out of the way and gain top spot.

"It was the way you always want to dream to win the title: to deserve to win and not just be gifted it," Harris says. "Frankie put me away in the European but I managed to keep going and come back through. I wasn't interested in racing for the rest of the day. The first title was a massive weight off my shoulders."

Harris' trips to the continent are rarely dull – this was Warneton in 2008

Momentum started to build. Success breeds success. Three weeks later, Harris crossed the English Channel to compete in the World Cup at Venray in the Netherlands.

"It was completely unexpected to win the World Cup. I had a terrible Saturday night, all sorts of hassle from the Dutch in scrutineering: cut this off your car, this is too wide. I let everybody have it on the first corner. And I couldn't quite believe it – I was racing for the top positions."

Harris moved up from the sixth row to fourth place on the first lap. Then he gradually reeled in fellow Brits Lee Fairhurst and Luke Davidson before passing Geert-Jan Keijzer to take the win.

Harris didn't finish the 2012 World Final at Skegness – nothing unusual in that, most of the top drivers didn't – but he wasn't finished winning trophies yet. The best season of his career so far was topped off with the silver roof, winning the National Points Shootout courtesy of some strong showings in the early rounds.

"It was lovely to win, but I went in with the attitude of, 'if I win I win, if I don't it's not the end of the world.' It made a big difference because I drove with my head. I won the Shootout and the grading points as well. I was having a bit of a ding dong at the time with Frankie, he tried burying me in the Grand National Championship at Belle Vue, but I won that as well. So it was a good season!"

Harris followed up his magnificent year by retaining the World Cup in Holland with another great first lap, moving up from the sixth row to second place in the carnage of the first few laps. Yet Harris found himself the object of attention off the track and in the pits again.

"That was a farce. On Saturday night, the day before the World Cup, I won the meeting final. They took the trophies off me and said, 'we'll present them to you tomorrow.' I didn't think anything of it and went to the scales – and what a joke that was. They reckoned that the car was too low. The ruler went under, but it scraped the floor of the sump guard. They said that there has to be a tolerance, so we asked to see it in the rulebook. We measured the ruler and it was a 53mm spirit level, not a 50mm one – that's why it was scraping. They packed the scales away and wouldn't weigh the car – that's it, I was out of the results. The next day, after winning the World Cup, I went to the scales. Everything was exactly the same as Saturday night, and they passed it!"

Harris was beginning to form the impression that, as the fastest driver in the fastest car, his opponents were resorting to underhand methods to stop him. Allegations arose that he was using traction control and illegal parts. He felt that he was unnecessarily banned for an off-season, off-track incident. When he won the World Final soon after retaining the World Cup, it seemed to get even worse.

As the sixtieth season dawned, Harris was enjoying racing under the gold roof, no longer feeling that he needed to prove himself in terms of results. But there is no doubt that he was becoming increasingly frustrated with the authorities in the sport and their off-the-track shenanigans. It bubbled over at the European Championship.

"The week before the European, I had a load of whingers trying to ban my tarmac car because of the axle," Harris says. "It states in the rulebook that you can use a Ford nine-inch centre section, which mine is. They said that because it's a trial axle I shouldn't be allowed to use it. But Craig Finnikin won the National Points with the same axle. He's had two podiums in the World Final with the same axle. So how come he can use it, but not me?"

In the Trust Fund race, the first of the European Championship weekend, Harris' frustration started to get the better of him when he found himself behind committee member Mat Newson.

"Newson gave me a massive hit the lap before and wouldn't come past so he had to have it."

Newson was sent flying; Josh Smith and Frankie Wainman Junior were collateral damage. Harris went on to finish fourth and win the meeting final but the ill-feeling with Newson – a figure of authority in terms of the technical car-building regulations – would run and run.

"I was adamant that I was going to win that, to stick two fingers up. I was pissed off, I was very pissed off."

Does Harris feel picked on?

"Yes, very much so. It's not just the cars that I build, it's my *own* car. Paul Ford bought my tarmac car, the one that I won the World Cup in twice. We both went to Venray. Bearing in mind that every time I went over, they scrutineered it to death. I had to cut this off it, cut that off it, alter this, change that, just to pass scrutineering. And every year we did it. This year we went across with my new car. It took us 45 minutes to get through scrutineering. Paul Ford was in scrutineering queue behind us, in my old car – straight through, they didn't even take the bonnet off, not bothered."

They say revenge is sometimes a dish best served cold, but that's not always the case. An hour or two after Newson was bashed, Harris was sent fencewards by Dan Johnson and Danny Wainman in the Grand National. He had a sleepless night as he prepared his car for the following day's European Championship. That race, in almost exactly the same place as the night before, Mat Newson rifled him back into the Armco, scraping the underside and rolling, causing yet more damage.

The tit-for-tat hits might have been over, but for Harris, the underlying reasons were still there.

"They don't like the fact that I'm young, I can build a car and win what I want with it. Some people say I've moved the sport on, some people say that I'm ruining the sport. But the cars have got bumpers on. They say it should be stock cars not racing cars, but as long as they've got a bumper on it isn't going to be a racing car. They keep whinging. Well, my answer to that is to get off the phone, go into the garage and make your car faster. And when they do, they don't want it back. Mat Newson has pulled off a number of times this year when I've got behind him. I haven't done half of what he's done to me, yet. They can't take it. In the Shootout, I was adamant that Dan Johnson and Mat Newson weren't going to win, and they didn't. If I hadn't buried Mat at Birmingham, he'd have been in a better shout of winning. While those two keep doing what they're doing, mouthing off, they'll never win another championship as long as I've got anything to do with it."

It's fighting talk, but it's a sign of his frustration. Part of the problem is that Tom Harris has a fundamentally different view of the sport than many other drivers out there. If he was to be given sole control for a period of time, there's no doubt that things would change – but he is aware that many others would disagree with him.

"They are supposed to be *Formula 1* stock cars. The ultimate. It wants to go more professional. Yes, it's a hobby for everybody, but people are so blind to the benefits. As soon as you mention using aluminium parts, they think cost, it's ex-

European weekend, Saturday: Harris gives spectators an unusual view

European weekend, Sunday: The trick is repeated...

...but this time the landing isn't quite so soft

pensive. It's not. Those people don't know, they don't look into it, they don't go to America. It's like wheels. The wheels on my tarmac car are half the price of getting somebody to make one for me. They come powder-coated black, out of the box, just put a tube and a tyre on it and go racing. If somebody makes one, it's double the cost. You've got to powder coat or anodize it, that's more money on top. People need to open their eyes. They're already making racing products, so why not just buy them? Some people haven't got time to spend making them, and it's cheaper to buy anyway. It would level the playing field; it would level the sport up no end."

Formula 1 stock car's heritage and history is that of a working man's sport. For decades, mechanics and farmers, scrap merchants and salesmen came together with self-built cars. Yet, according to Harris, the sport has outgrown that. Trying to get F1 stock cars to return to that kind of approach would be like asking Andy Murray and Rafael Nadal to start using a wooden racket.

"They keep on about stock parts for stock cars. But they aren't stock parts. My tarmac car probably has more stock parts on it than any other car on the track. You can ring up and buy them off the shelf. It's not a bespoke part made for a racing car, which is what everybody else is using. If they say you've got to use a stock transit hub, well, it's got drum brakes on it. Who uses drum brakes in a stock car? Nobody. So they'd rather spend four hours in the garage making a new hub. That isn't a stock part. But I can ring America and have a new hub here in three days. And it's still cheaper than getting somebody to make one. It's wrong."

Harris' vision for the future is one which embraces professionalism and a new way of doing things. It's a view which was strengthened after securing the opportunity to race in the United States in early 2015 and seeing first-hand how oval racing is organised across the Atlantic.

"It's been brewing for a couple of years," Harris says. "It's something I've always wanted to have a go and do. I went to Smiley Sitton's Race School in Florida to drive a World of Outlaw sprint car. He was really impressed with me, he couldn't believe it. His mechanics said that it was the first time he hasn't been screaming down the radio at a new driver! They were moving the wing and changing shockers, they were bolting brand new tyres on. That never happens so soon. I was on the pace, so he asked us to go back out and race."

A couple of weeks before the NFL Superbowl, American midget racing's equivalent is held on a specially-laid indoor dirt track in Tulsa, Oklahoma: the Chili Bowl. It's competed for over five nights, each of which has 15,000 enthusiastic spectators in the stands. Competitors include stars of NASCAR, drag racing, IndyCar – and, in 2015, Formula 1 stock cars.

"I had the chance of a free car but it wasn't a top car, it was just a car to go racing in. A bit like Mat Newson's hire cars, and no disrespect, but you're not going to choose to go out in the World Final in one of those. Instead I got an almost brand-new car which has done five meetings from Bob East, one of the best car builders in the States."

Considering it was his first outing in the biggest midget car championship of them all, Harris performed admirably. In a complicated scoring system, he competed in the in the C-Feature on his qualifying night, finishing ninth out of fourteen starters, and in the J-Feature on championship night, finishing seventh out of sixteen. Seeing the slick American organisation and PR machine at work made Harris realise the extent of the contrast with his home formula.

"The sport is professionally run by independent people. It's a massive business and it's run properly."

It's pretty clear that Harris thinks the style of organisation and administration that he saw in the US could do wonders for his own formula back in the UK. But, much as he has his disagreements with the governing bodies, Harris is not about to walk away from Formula 1 stock cars – probably.

"I'm not going to sell my stock car stuff, I'm not going to give them the satisfaction of beating me, but if I can go and race in America and race rather than build stock cars for a job then I'll do it. I'd love to race in the World of Outlaws, that's the top of the tree on dirt ovals. It's going to be no easy ride to get there but if I've got an opportunity then I'll grab it with both hands."

Anyway, Harris still has things left to do in F1.

"Any championship would be awesome to win," Harris says, "but I really want to win the British, it's the only thing I've not won. I've had a lot of bad luck in past British Championships. In 2013, I started on pole but got a puncture. I started on the front row at King's Lynn in 2011 but didn't get round the first corner. I got into the lead at Belle Vue in 2009 and the half shaft went. The World Final win meant a lot too, so I'd love to win that again to show that it wasn't a fluke."

Tom Harris might be a bit of a dreamer. His chances of finding employment as a professional racing driver in the States might be slim. But others have been there before him: Dan Wheldon, Dario Franchitti, Nigel Mansell. And if his personal ambitions don't work out, what about his hopes for Formula 1 stock cars? Perhaps one day, Harris' suggestions will be taken on board and Formula 1 stock car racing will no longer be a poor and distant cousin of World of Outlaws or even Formula 1 Grand Prix.

As Harris says: "You've got to be ambitious to get to the top."

Remarkable rollovers

Two rollovers in two days was good going from Tom Harris. But spectacular accidents are not unusual in Formula 1 stock cars...

Rob Cowley attempts the stock car high jump record

You're supposed to go around them, not over them

Frankie Wainman Junior escapes serious injury at Hednesford

An interesting way to
sneak through the gap

Barry Sheene would be
impressed with this wheelie

It's not just Brits who do
spectacular crashes – the
Dutch are good at it too

Hmm, will a tractor or crane
be needed? Or both?

EUROPEAN CHAMPION
& GRAND NATIONAL

515

FRANKIE WAINMAN JUNIOR

Thirteen National Points Championships, seven British Championships, three European Championships. Two World Final wins, six international World Championships. More than one thousand race wins, a quarter of which of which have been meeting finals. Make no mistake – Frankie Wainman Junior is a stock car legend.

He was brought up in a successful stock car family. It's been his passion and his job for more than two decades. He met his wife at the racetrack, his children have followed in his footsteps and jumped behind the wheel. If you chopped Frankie Wainman Junior in half, like a stick of rock, it would say "Formula 1 stock cars".

His life is so intertwined with stock cars that's it's difficult to imagine stock cars without him, or him without stock cars. What exactly would Wainman be doing if he wasn't a stock car driver?

"How would I know that?" Wainman laughs. "It's been my life for virtually all my life. I was born into it. My dad raced, he started the year that I was born so I went to my first meeting when I was ten days old. I haven't missed many since then!"

Frankie Wainman Senior was a popular driver in the 1970s, a golden decade for Formula 1 stock cars. He duelled with Stuart Smith, Willie Harrison, Dave Chisholm, Doug Cronshaw and Mike Close among others – a time when many fans would say that the sport was at its peak.

"Dad first went to watch stock cars at Nelson," Wainman says. "At that time he was big into tractors, breaking them up and selling them. He looked at the stock cars that were out there and thought, 'I can do something better than that.' He built his first car – he didn't buy one, he built his own straight away – and it wasn't that bad really. He did alright."

Frankie Senior soon got up to red top and by the mid-seventies was challenging for honours. He won the World Championship at White City in 1979. When Stuart Smith cut back the amount he raced after 1981, the way was clear for new drivers to claim the silver roof. Frankie Senior was one of the beneficiaries, winning the title in 1984, 1985 and 1986. He was certainly due a win – no driver has finished second in the National Points Championship on more occasions. And, all the time, young Frankie was there, taking it all in, slowly learning the ropes.

"I was fetched up with it. I went to every meeting, worked on my dad's cars. I looked after them the year he won the National Points Championship. That was my job, doing everything, swapping axles and getting ready for racing."

By that point, Frankie Junior had already got his own racing career under way.

"I started in Ministox in 1981. The Minis were hard; my dad didn't have the money or time to help me with them. He was getting involved with exporting tractors to Pakistan, which took over from milking on the farm, and he was racing himself. Back then they were proper Minis. They were old shit things! We were still going the opposite way round. The last year or so that I raced, Martin O'Neill took me on and kept my car. He came to every meeting with me. I was one of the very first to put the seat in the middle, that was so I could reach the pedals properly, but it was nothing like the Ministox are now."

Having grown up around Formula 1 stock cars, helped his father with the spanners and raced in Ministox, there was no question that Wainman was going to carry on his racing career after he turned sixteen. He was desperate to start as soon as possible. Five days after his birthday, he rolled out on track at Long Eaton in a new self-built car. He failed to make an impression in wet and muddy conditions, but the following day at Aycliffe, he registered top-five finishes in each of his four races. His third meeting at Crewe was even better – three races, three top-three placings, one of which was his maiden race win.

It was the first of many. Frankie debuted at the tail end of the 1987 season but still managed to pick up eleven wins over the final month, including two heat and final doubles. He ended the season as a blue top, but with the fifth-best points-per-meeting average.

Wainman was probably the highest-profile novice the sport had ever seen and he coped with it admirably. The pressure of a famous family name was like water off a duck's back. However, it wasn't all plain sailing.

Frankie, Frankie and Phoebe in 2004 – two generations of the Racing Wainmans

"It all went a bit pear-shaped when my mum and dad split up soon after I started. My dad and I didn't talk for a lot of years, not properly. Because we fell out, I had to get my own transport to race meetings. It wasn't a nice period, but you just get on with it. I left school and did an apprenticeship which seemed like the right thing to do at the time, but with hindsight maybe it wasn't. I served my time and got my qualifications, but I was on crap money for four years and it didn't change what I was going to do. I always knew I was going to build stock cars."

As soon as his apprenticeship was complete, Wainman started spending as much time as possible in his workshop, building stock cars for himself and for paying customers. It would become his full-time job for more than two decades, and he is still going strong.

"I've had some top drivers in my cars who have won championships," Wainman says. "Paul Hines was racing one of mine when he won the European Championship. Paul Harrison won heat and final first time out in his new tarmac car. I built Rob Speak's car and he won the European Championship, first time out in it – I got second. As the race was finishing, I thought to myself, 'I could have won that if I hadn't built his car!' He had the best that I could give him. But I was pleased from a construction point of view."

Well, that's one way to make sure Andy Smith doesn't recognise you!

Building and maintaining a fleet of stock cars is a time-consuming profession. From early morning, Wainman can be found in his workshop with only his dogs for company. What he has to do depends on what has happened at the weekend. If a driver has suffered significant damage, his car might be left with Wainman on the understanding that it'll be fixed by the following meeting. If there are no urgent repair jobs, new cars are constructed for drivers who want them. If time permits, he might be working on son Frankie's Ministox or daughter Phoebe's V8 Hotstox. Only if all other tasks are complete can Wainman focus on his own car.

"Every week varies," Wainman says. "I try to work on a car, load it for the weekend, and then get the next one out. I'll usually be trying to build one new one too. There isn't a lot of room. I work right through. If the lads come up to work on my cars I won't break off to help them, they know that I have to work to pay for everything. I'll work alongside them on customer's stuff while they work on my cars. That's the way it's got to be. We don't have any funding. I'm up there until ten or half ten but have Wednesday nights off. Some days I'll stop for tea and watch *Emmerdale*!"

Hailing from rural West Yorkshire, there's no other viewing option for the Wainman household. They're all avid fans and Wainman has met some of its stars.

"Lucy Pargeter, who plays Chastity Dingle, raced one of my hire cars in a demo race in 2006. She came up and was supposed to have a practice in the car in the driveway. She set off down the lane, turned out and shot off towards the village! I was stood with her boyfriend, Rudi Coleano, he was laughing. I said, 'What are you laughing at, you need to go and get her!' But he was in his brand new BMW so I had to jump in my car and chase her down the road. I passed two cars so she must have passed them too! She had pulled up in a gateway, nearly in the village, I could hear her laughing. She said, 'I'm practising, you told me to practice!'"

It was a little surprising that it took Wainman five years from his F1 debut to capture a major championship, the British, won at Coventry in 1992. After that, the floodgates opened. Wainman won the National Points Championship in 1994, losing it to Andy Smith in 1995 in a tight three-way race with John Lund that went down to the last meeting of the season. The 1995 European Championship was some compensation for losing the silver roof, which Wainman regained in 1996.

"I knew that I was in there with all the top lads and that I could beat them all, but it's down to luck on the day and if your equipment keeps together. I was in the top three in the National Points with Peter Falding and John Lund for a couple of years before I won it, but it was hard work. They were so much better than everybody else. I struggled with engines but didn't have any money, so we made do with what we had."

Then followed a period of utter domination. From 1996 to 2009, Wainman topped the grading points list at the end of every season. The silver-roofed 515 car became a fixture for more than a decade on the racetrack, only absent in 1998 and 2005 because the gold roof of the World Champion took precedence.

"Winning the National Points Championship was all about dedication, doing the meetings, and consistency in races," Wainman says. "When I look back at the races that I won then, it was every meeting – big numbers."

Forty, fifty, sixty race wins a season were common. Such was his margin of victory – typically having the National Points title in the bag by the World Final – that the rules were altered to give the rest of the grid a fighting chance of competing with Wainman. The silver roof was transferred to the National Series, with qualifying points raced for over a limited amount of meetings. It didn't really make any difference – over the seven years that the silver roof was raced for under this format, Wainman won six and came second to Andy Smith in the other.

Only when the Shootout was introduced in 2009, when the number of qualifying meetings was reduced again, was the silver roof taken away from Wainman for good. Ironically, that's pretty much the same time that Wainman stopped topping the grading points list, meaning that the silver roof would have gone to a different driver anyway.

"It was very raw to start with when they first introduced the National Series," Wainman reveals. "I knew it was just to stop me winning the silver roof. The

One of the many 515 cars to have carried the silver roof

Shootout is brilliant, I enjoy being in it, I can't say that I don't. I firmly believe that the Shootout winner should have the silver roof. But he isn't the National Points Champion. I said quite a few years ago, when this all kicked off, that it wouldn't be until the likes of Tom Harris and Mat Newson start winning the grading points that they'll realise they haven't got anything for it. The 2014 grading points went to one point and I was only 54 behind that, but nobody knew about it. I honestly don't get it. It's there. We're all in it. Why not make something of it? It has a status. It always will have. To me, the National Points Champion is the person who does all the meetings and gets all the points."

After Wainman's last official silver roof in 2008 and unofficial grading points title in 2009, there was a drop off in his performances. True, over a four-year period he still finished second in the National Points Shootout twice and earned two podiums in both the World and British Championships. Yet, for a man so accustomed to success, it seemed like slim pickings. What had changed?

"Back when I was winning, we didn't have big flash engines. We made do, bits of sponsorship kept us going. Now they have new engines costing £30,000 from the USA. I don't know where all that came from or if we need it."

Wainman felt that he was priced out of the running, but he feels that new rules and regulations regarding shock absorbers have levelled the playing field and negated the ability of certain drivers to buy success.

Silver roof no more, but Wainman still has the superstar's flashing amber lights

"The main difference this season has been the new shockers. I've never spent money on shockers, partly because I couldn't and partly because I didn't want to. I mistakenly didn't realise exactly what the top lads were spending on them, they were spending an awful lot of money. What I didn't find out was that they were spending three hundred quid on an eighty quid shocker to get it sorted. Now that we're all on the same control shocker, it's been proved that is where my car used to let down. It was instant."

Wainman felt like he was back on the pace, particularly leading up to the European Championship weekend.

"The tarmac car was really good. We worked a little bit more on it, got to Northampton for practice on Saturday afternoon and it was the quickest car, quicker than Tom Harris. That was proved by the fact that Tom smashed it up in the first race. Tom followed Mat Newson straight into me. Absolutely wrecked it. Ripped axles out of it and everything. The Saturday night before the European Championship race, somebody always smashes it up. The team and I did an awesome job putting it back together and I was straight back out for the consolation with no wing on. It wasn't that bad. Once you lose your base settings you lose your way a bit. Once you smash every corner out, you don't know where you are. But we got it back somewhere very near."

All the hours of preparation, all the weeks spent honing the car, could have been spoiled by one crash. But Wainman's experience, together with that of his mechanic team, meant that they worked methodically and with an eye for detail.

"The team found another shocker that was slightly bent the next morning – when you're rushing to get it back out, you can miss things like that. But I was still in bed in the coach. I couldn't move. It hurt!"

The European Championship is raced for over a graded start. Wainman took up his usual position with the superstars at the back, his younger brother Danny was in with the red tops. But it was a closed grid – the gaps between yellow, blue, red and superstars were missing.

"In the big races, I know if I want to do any good I've got to do a lot of cars straight away. I think I passed fourteen red tops on one corner. I laced the lot of them. I came out behind Danny who was going from the middle of the red tops – he said to me he double-looked in his mirrors, he couldn't believe I was there. I had the quickest car in the race, everything was right it, just felt perfect. It was real good. I knew that it was quicker than Danny's."

The Wainman brothers circulated for five laps, picking off those in front, before Frankie took his brother for fifth place. Now Danny followed Frankie for fifteen laps, until Frankie bumpered Shaun Blakemore out of the way. The brothers were first and second. It should have been an easy cruise for a Wainman one-two, but Mat Newson chose that moment to rifle Tom Harris hard into the fence, leading to waved yellow flags and a temporary stoppage.

"That's what you really don't want," Wainman says. "I've always set my tarmac car to come on at the end of the race on tarmac. It was a joy to drive and I was enjoying it. But when I realised it was Tom Harris who was upside down, I thought, 'well, that'll do me!'"

The yellow flags had bunched the field back up again. Danny was right on Frankie's back bumper, but of more concern to Frankie was Rob Speak, lurking in third position. Thankfully, there were no problems on the restart and the Wainmans were able to get away from danger to take the chequered flag.

"Danny knew full well that if he messed about, Speaky would win it," Wainman says. "He knew that we had to get away or we both would have been put in."

But why didn't Danny use his bumper to take dispose of his older brother and the title?

"Because he knew I would have got him back," Wainman says, "and I would have done! My car doesn't go into the wall, it comes out and kills whatever it gets put in by, and that's how I've always been. I'd won the race at the start. Whether that played in his head a little bit I don't know. Danny wasn't quick enough. But we had a first and a second which was awesome. You can't get better than that."

The evening before the
European Championship,
Wainman has some repairs
to do

But with a new wing,
Wainman scythes
through the field

Crossing the line in a
Wainman one-two, both
brothers smoke their tyres
in celebration

Wainman's first major
title since 2008

Looking good with red and yellow checks

As Wainman's first major championship title since the National Series in 2008, there's no doubt that all the waiting made this victory taste particularly sweet.

"It was a good weekend. Yes, I know I got smashed up on Saturday night, but the team put it back together well. I'd only won the European twice before, it's a hard one to win from superstar. Usually you'll get an oddball who wins it from the front of a grade. The number of years that I've come second and third to yellow tops and blue tops... you just can't catch them. Whenever that happens, there's never a yellow. Whenever I'm winning, there is a yellow! But everybody wants to win it. Andy Smith never did – and I stopped him quite a few times."

Andy Smith – he was bound to be mentioned at some point. No other driver has tormented Wainman more. The two clashed as early as the fight for the National Points Championship in 1995, but it was a decade later when it really started to get personal. The bitter rivalry was captured by BBC cameras during the 2009 season for the television series *Gears and Tears*, instantly transforming the rivalry into the most famous in the history of F1 stock cars. So there's no surprise that it's with a hint of pride that Wainman notes he has won the European Championship three times while Smith won none.

"He's never won the European. I stopped him twice or three times on purpose because of stuff that he's done to me, taking me out. Now he's never won it and never will."

Smith aside, Wainman has had more than his fair share of rivalries over the years.

"Where do you start?" Wainman smiles. "I've had that many. Gaz Bott, Chris Elwell, Peter Falding. John Lund, Rob Speak, Andy Smith. You go on and on and on. Tom Harris, Dan Johnson, Ryan Harrison."

Why do they pick on Wainman?

"If I knew that I'd be sorted. I don't know why Tom Harris picked me. Probably because I was one of the best and he wanted to have a go. I don't think I was much of a threat to him, but obviously I was. Ryan Harrison was the same. I've watched Ryan physically lock both wheels up so he didn't hit Tom Harris when he's been passed by him, then I've passed him and he's put me in. What was that all about? Why? But I'll take on whatever comes; I'm not bothered in the slightest. I knocked Tom out of the British Championship at Buxton in 2013. He told people he just needed to turn up and get the trophy. No Tom, it doesn't work like that."

Maybe there's an alternative reason. Does Wainman pick on them? Does he bring it on himself?

"I don't pick on anybody! Simple as that," Wainman responds – perhaps a little too quickly!

It's likely that new, upcoming drivers like to make a statement by taking on the established name in the formula. For the last two decades, that name has been Frankie Wainman Junior, so it's hardly surprising that nearly every major rivalry has involved him. Sometimes it pays off for the young gun, but often it backfires.

"I remember Stuart Smith Junior putting me in the fence at Skegness one night in 2004. It was his first full year. The next day, I put him in proper in the first race and he was a mess. His dad came up to me in the pits – Stuart Senior was a man of few words with me and I thought this could be a bit dodgy – and he said, 'Well done! He deserved it!' He saw it as it was, you can't say more than that!"

Back to the 2014 season, and Wainman continued to stick with the pace after repainting his roof with the red and yellow checks of the European Champion. He stood an outside chance of returning the silver roof to its spiritual home in Silsden until he was accidentally taken out by his brother in one of the heats of the Shootout finale. That left one last title to fight for: the Grand National Championship, awarded to the driver who scores the most points in Grand National races throughout the season.

"You know the ones that are going for it," Wainman says. "Mat Newson steps up in Grand Nationals, so do Tom Harris and Danny. There are only a few who will ever win it. By the end, there was only me and Mat in it. There was just one point in it, I just had to beat him, but I nearly didn't get in the race after Danny drove me into a post. We cobbled the car back together but the front left suspension was all naff. The steering arm, which bolts through the track rod end, hadn't been drilled out. The marshals were waiting for me to go out on track. I was in the car. All the team had to do was bolt the track rod on, but they couldn't do it. I got it wrong in my head what they were doing, told them to do something that was wrong, and it got stuck. They couldn't do anything. But I had to be in the race, I just had to beat Mat. I was getting proper stressed. The air was turning blue inside the cab! We basically got the track rod onto the bolt and wrapped it on with tie wraps. I didn't have a choice."

Luckily for Wainman, Newson's attention was elsewhere. While Wainman managed to get away and creep around for fifth place, Newson trailed behind in ninth. The bodged repair job withstood the stresses placed on it by the Sheffield shale.

"It stopped together, even after the race. My dad had a look afterwards and just shook his head and laughed."

The victory made it ten Grand National titles for Wainman – his second-most successful championship after the National Points. They sit alongside 25 major UK championships and a whole host of other minor championship trophies. Yet, despite the fact that he ruled British stock cars for so long, when Wainman is asked about his best achievements, it's all about the titles he has won abroad.

"The foreign titles are harder to win," Wainman says. "My best achievement was winning the Long Track Championship in the Netherlands in 1998. To win that with the equipment that I had was a buzz. I had the shale engine in my tarmac car. I think we went to every Baarlo meeting that year because I wanted to win it, but we blew the engine up the meeting before. We fixed it and I beat Ron Kroonder. Didn't smash him up, but actually beat him. I did enjoy that. I'd love to race the engine that I've got now on the long track. It was awesome."

Alongside that final Long Track Championship, Wainman has twice won its replacement, the World Cup, alongside three World 240 Championships in New Zealand. To go to foreign fields and return home with their premier title is something which takes a lot of guts – especially in New Zealand, the home of rough, aggressive racing.

"They don't like you to go down there and win," Wainman says, "especially the first time. There were six of them after me. The buzz that gave me to win – I'll never match it."

Why doesn't Wainman rank his two World Final wins up there with his best wins?

"I got put off the World Final in 1994. My engine blew up when I should have won it. That disappointment – I never want that again. It was probably the lowest point of my career."

The annual New Zealand trip – a highlight in Wainman's year

Wainman's radiator fan sheared a hose early in the 1994 World Final and, although he led for twelve laps, with three to go his engine seized. Wainman was heartbroken and sought solace in future years by dedicating himself to the National Points Championship – a season-long competition that could not be lost due to a single mechanical malfunction – rather than the World Championship.

"We'd done everything right but a failure just happened. So I don't build myself up for it. If I win it, I win it. If I don't, I don't. It's never had a lot of interest for me if I'm honest. It's just one race."

That won't stop the legion of Wainman fans from living in hope every September. Every year he seems to be there – he has only missed two World Finals in 27 years – but he has won just two. It's perhaps the only statistic in Wainman's racing career that is a little disappointing. Yet there are thousands of fans out there who want to see him win another to join the elite club of six drivers with three or more World Championship titles. Is Wainman aware that he has so many fans and followers?

"Yes, one hundred per cent. It's what keeps me racing. It worries me a little bit that the young kids don't get much of a fan base. I don't know why. It's still me, John Lund and Paul Harrison who have the biggest fan bases, and it shouldn't be really. It should be Tom Harris, Dan Johnson, Mat Newson, the young drivers coming through. They are not getting the fans and I don't know why."

The family name is part of the answer. Wainman inherited some supporters from his dad, who was a popular driver. Over more than two decades he has picked up many more fans – the Wainman truck is always surrounded by well-wishers in the pits. It's a popularity which has been passed down another generation – Frankie Junior Junior is the biggest name in Ministox, Phoebe is the most well-known in V8 Hotstox. Both will have to find a way to cope with the pressure of living up to the family name, as their father has done.

Phoebe and young Frankie's racing careers will give their dad an outlet for when he stops racing. Not that he has any plans to hang up his helmet any time in the future.

"I'll be dead before I retire," Wainman laughs. "Until I get to the point that I'm rubbish, and people tell me that I'm rubbish, I'll want to keep racing. My dad retired when he was still getting top ten finishes and he was still competitive. I told him I thought he could carry on, but he said that it seemed like the right time to stop. Maybe that will happen to me, but I'm not there yet. It's never crossed my mind. While I'm doing something I enjoy, why stop doing it?"

Wainman probably has more competition now than he ever had during his career – and remember that he had some ding-dong battles with John Lund, Rob Speak and Andy Smith. But it would be a brave man who bet against him adding a third World Championship, making it to double figures in the British Championship, or making history by taking a fourteenth National Points Championship.

Triple World Champion

He has won many titles over many seasons, but if there was a single year that was Wainman's best, it must be 1998. Aside from winning the National Points Championship (again), Benevolent Fund trophy and Grand Prix Series, Wainman managed the incredible feat of collecting three different World Championship titles from around the world.

January: 240 World Championship, Palmerston North, New Zealand
Wainman became the second UK driver to win the premier Kiwi Superstocks title. In the final race, he effectively had a massive target on his back bumper – none of the natives wanted to see him take the title. But, despite their best efforts, Wainman escaped their clutches for the first of his three titles Down Under.

August: Long Track World Championship, Baarlo, Netherlands

Racing under a specially designed wing almost double the usual size, Wainman won the last Long Track Championship before the kilometre-long Baarlo oval closed. He earned the title by passing reigning champion Louw Wobbes and five-times champion Ron Kroonder. Rather than beating them with the bumper, Wainman beat the Dutch at their own game.

September: World Championship, Coventry, UK
Possibly the most controversial World Final ever, Wainman won the race after main rival John Lund was taken out by lap-down New Zealander, Stan Hickey. The fact that Hickey was racing a car borrowed from Wainman led to accusations of cheating and team racing. The resulting fallout helped to sour Wainman's relationship with the UK-based World Championship.

16
MAT NEWSON

Mat Newson: the nearly man. Of the active Formula 1 stock car drivers who started the sixtieth season, only Mark Gilbank had won more races and finals without taking a major championship trophy – and he started amassing his total of race wins ten years earlier.

Is Mat Newson the best driver not to have won one of the big four – World, British, European or National Points Championships?

"I regularly get reminded that I've not won a major championship, but so have a lot of people," Newson says. "There are one hundred people in this sport and 95% of them have never won anything, but they've never been close to it either. I think people judge me on that a lot more because I'm always so close. I'm nearly there, that's why I get reminded. I've been at the top end of the sport for a long time."

To be fair, Newson is not alone. There have been some excellent drivers in the history of the sport who have won more meeting finals but did not win a major championship: Gaz Bott, Mick Noden and Bobby Burns among them. It's a club of illustrious drivers, but Newson's aim is to get out of it as soon as possible.

His desire for a major title began as a result of his father's interest in motor-sport. Robin Newson was racing driver who passed on the need for speed to his son.

"Racing has been in the family since before I was born," Newson says. "It's been like that ever since, we've never been out of it. My dad was racing bangers when I was born. In the early nineties, he decided that he'd had enough of the banger scene and wanted to race Formula 1 stock cars. He bought a Formula 1 from John Lawn, who was the closest driver around here, and went racing. He went with Paul Corker, who also lived round here and started about the same time, but they probably only raced once a month – it was a very low key thing."

Growing up around cars and around the racetrack meant that young Mat was desperate to have a go behind the wheel himself.

"I turned ten and my dad bought me an ORC Ministox. Almost straight away, he decided that he would only go racing when I didn't. His Formula 1 career didn't take off mainly because I was racing Ministox nearly every weekend and every Thursday. I was National Points Champion and won most championships, probably nearly every track championship we raced. I was very successful in the later years, just before I finished, although when I started at ten I was not very good at all – it was quite embarrassing!"

Already, some of the traits that would characterise Newson's later racing career were beginning to show themselves.

"A lot of the success came from the amount of time we spent on the car. My dad would make sure that the car was always spot on and if he thought there was an advantage to be gained by doing something he would do it. Then the second I left school at half past three, I would go and work on them too. And you get better the more practice you do. We used to race twice on a Sunday; we'd race at midday at Bovingdon in London, then Yarmouth on Sunday night. The more you do the better you get."

When Newson turned sixteen, his father stepped aside and Mat inherited his stock car. He wanted to get behind the wheel as soon as possible, although there was a false start before he got going.

"My sixteenth birthday was the day that Rob Speak won the 2001 World Final. I went to Hednesford that day to buy a couple of new tyres because I was going to race a Formula 1 the following week. But, on the night of the World Final, I raced my last Ministox meeting at Wimbledon. I had a few scores to settle and got banned! So my first ever meeting came at Northampton."

Newson's career in F1 got under way, a month later than planned, on a special occasion – the 500th Formula 1 stock car meeting in the UK. It is a meeting that will be remembered for the debut of not just one future superstar, but two.

"It was the first ever go in Formula 1 for Stuart Smith Junior too," Newson recalls. "Looking back, the equipment I had was shocking but I had to start somewhere. I had my dad's old car, Stuart had Andy Smith's car! I started from the back and didn't do any good at all. Then I went to King's Lynn and Sheffield the following week, and Stoke the week after that, then the season was over. I did better on shale because I could with the equipment that I had."

Gotta start somewhere!

Newson picked up his first top ten race finishes at Sheffield and Stoke but he still started the following season as a wet-behind-the-ears novice. He decided to use his father's car only on shale and started building a new car for tarmac, which made its debut at the European Championship meeting almost halfway through the season. It picked up a fifth place finish on its first appearance, his second-best result at the time.

Newson went from white to yellow after a couple of months and retained that grade for the rest of the season, taking his first race win on the Buxton tarmac in late September and the Novice of the Year title. The off season saw another new car being built in the Newson garage, this time a shale car to replace his dad's old thumper. That paid dividends almost immediately, with a consolation and final double at Sheffield in May which saw Newson get the blue paint out for the first time.

It wasn't a story of immediate success à la Frankie Wainman Junior. Newson climbed the grades slowly, gradually expanding and improving as time, experience and budget allowed.

"I didn't do much tarmac because I couldn't compete, I didn't have the equipment. Then I got a tarmac car and started to do a little more. But I spent those first two seasons with two cars and one engine, so I was picking and choosing my

Moving up the ladder... Newson joins the blues

meetings. I'd get a run of three tarmac meetings so I'd put the engine in the tarmac car. Then I'd get a run of shale meetings so I'd swap over."

The blue-roofed number 16 car was a standard fixture on the racetrack for the next few seasons. Newson was a fairly decent driver in fairly average cars, but it never seemed likely that he would have to invest in a set of flashing amber lights. Each year he would pick up a handful of wins, nothing more than you could count on one hand. And that's the way it looked like it was going to stay, until a stroke of good fortune kick-started his rise to the top.

"Probably the biggest single thing that changed my racing career was when Billy-Tom O'Connor gave me the car that he was racing. He'd just had a brand new car built and only raced it once, but to cut a long story short, he was emigrating and gave it to me. He came to see me one day to borrow a few parts, I didn't know anything about him but helped him out."

In April 2007, Newson was struggling at a tarmac weekend double-header. He finished third in his heat at the first meeting at Birmingham, but then a damaged differential threatened to put an end to both the Birmingham meeting and the following day at Hednesford.

"Billy came to see me at Birmingham and said, 'do you need a diff for that axle?' He didn't live very far away so I went back to his and picked it up. We got talking and got friendly. That week he rang me and told me about the car and said, 'come and have it, it's yours.' That gave me my first ever small-block engine which I used on tarmac. I didn't have to do any engine swapping any more. That was my big start, having two good cars and doing well. I used the car for two seasons, at the end of the second season I sold it to Colin Goodswen and sent the money to Billy. I got two years of use out of it for nothing, and he had somebody sort out selling the car, so he was well happy."

O'Connor's generous offer gave Newson the equipment he needed to move from being a blue top to a red top. Now he was a star driver, and another bit of fortune would boost him further.

"Around about that time when I sold Billy's car, my mechanic was friendly with Jamie Davidson. Luke was having a new one, so Jamie gave me Luke's car for nothing. Then a year or so later, Jamie said to me, 'why don't you come up and copy Luke's new car?' I had a really in-depth look and measured it as accurately as I could. Then I brought out a new tarmac car and it was a nigh-on exact copy. That set me from being an average red to being better. That's what I needed, a bit of advice with setup and car construction."

Newson has not been alone in benefiting from the goodwill of others. Stock car racing is a community-oriented sport. Drivers pitch in to give each other a hand, lending parts and helping out where they can. Spectators and fans will have a whip-round to help out a struggling driver who needs a specific part.

Perhaps O'Connor and Davidson recognised Newson's potential and respected his sense of hard work. Right from the start, ever since he had sat behind the wheel of a Ministox, Newson was prepared to devote time and hard graft to his racing. Few drivers raced in more meetings that he did. Certainly nobody put in more miles on the road. Based in Norfolk, Newson faced four and five-hour trips most weekends. Nobody knew the A47 and A17 better than him.

"I just enjoy it," Newson explains. "I'd rather not be sitting on the internet looking at the results on a Saturday evening, I'd rather be there. We have to travel a lot of miles, but I'm fortunate that I work for myself. If I'm late home and don't want to go to work early in the morning, then I don't have to. I never set out at the start of the year and say that I'm doing them all regardless of what happens. But unless I'm hurt, injured or can't afford to, then I've got no reason not to race. My daughter absolutely loves it. She gives me a harder time if we don't go than I do!"

And then, when he gets back home, few drivers with full-time jobs put in the same number of hours as Newson does in the garage. He churns out a new car most winters while struggling to maintain the ones that he already has.

"I'm a mechanic by trade," Newson explains. "If you can fix a road car, you can fix a stock car. All I've done since I've left school is fix cars. I left school and got a job at a Mitsubishi dealer, did a five-year apprenticeship, got my qualifications and stayed there for a bit. Then my dad had a business which was growing quite well and needed some help. Working here for my dad seemed a far better idea at the time, but we didn't last long, just a few months! We didn't get on well working together, like any father and son. He said that he was thinking of moving on and doing something else so I bought the business off him and he started up a new one. We still work from the same premises but on two separate businesses so we don't argue now like we did when we were together. It works."

The aid that Newson received from benefactors like Billy-Tom O'Connor and Jamie Davidson was deserved. The impact was obvious. He jumped into the top ten of the grading list, going from a consistent blue top to a consistent superstar. Newson also began to expand his involvement in stock cars. Now he was going to help others out by running hire cars for those who wanted a one-off experience or for more regular drivers who needed a car for a specific meeting.

"I was fortunate that I didn't need to go and buy the cars to hire, I had them. Because of the generous help that I had from Billy-Tom and Jamie, I had two good cars. Then Steve Lewin, whose cars I used to look after, lost heart and decided he wanted out. He said that for everything I'd done for him, I could have the cars until I sold them. I had some very good equipment, but suddenly I had far more cars than I would ever be able to drive!"

They were sat in the Newson workshop, but they wouldn't be unused for long.

"Luke Davidson didn't have a shale car but there were a couple of World Championship qualifying rounds on shale, so I told him that I would sort out a shale car – his dad had done enough for me, so I wanted to help him. People saw that I had lent Luke a car, so asked if I would lend them one. Then I started advertising, saying that I would hire cars, and the phone was ringing all the time. I used one of Steve's cars for three or four seasons before I sold it and paid Steve. He got his money; I got a load of use out of the car first."

The hire cars became so successful that Newson's own form began to suffer.

"In 2013, it was nearly all I did. It was like a full-time job. I didn't have the best season myself and we put it down to the fact that I didn't touch my cars because I was working on the hire ones. I tell people that during a meeting my car comes first, but regular hirers, especially ones who have got their own pit crews, are ideal. I don't have to strap them in. They know what to do. Their crews know how to look after them. All they have to do is say that they need something, I'll tell them where it is, job done. The hardest drivers to look after are the first timers. By the time I've strapped them in, checked everything and made sure they are lined up; the next thing I know my race is going out on track!"

Not only was Newson building and maintaining his own cars and keeping his fleet of hire cars on track, he was also finding himself increasingly busy looking after other people's cars too.

Newson debuted this distinctively coloured tarmac car in 2011

Sometimes it was quick...

...sometimes not

But it all came to an abrupt and messy end at the 2013 British Championship

Two Newson cars – one for Mat, one for hire (in this case, by his dad!)

"I'm lucky that the premises that I work from is very big. Somebody asked me if I would repair their car. It doesn't matter to me whether it's a Ford Focus or a stock car. Everybody pays the same kind of money! That took off. You put the word about a bit, and the next thing you know I had endless people wanting a new car. Can you repair this? Can you modify it? That took over a massive part of my life. I don't do it full time but sometimes it feels like I do."

Newson is kept busy between race meetings, but helping to fix and maintain other people's cars has had a positive impact on his own fabrication.

"I've been lucky that a lot of people I've been involved with had different cars. I had a period where I looked after Jonathan Lewis' car and he had a Wainman-build. It lived in my workshop so I'd have a look and think, that's how Frankie does it. I had copied Luke Davidson's car so I knew how Cecil did it. The next thing, I had a Peter Falding car that I looked after, so that's how Peter did it. Then I looked after Scott Davids' cars. Between all of them, by taking a bit of everything and using what I think are the best bits of all of them, I can build what I consider to be a decent car."

Newson's most recent creations started the 2014 season well. Nine podium finishes in the first eight meetings of the season saw him rise to the top of the grading chart for the first time at the end of the first grading period, while the UK Open

Championship a couple of weeks later had Newson leading until the unstoppable Stuart Smith Junior caught him with five laps to go.

"Stuart made the right tyre choice but I didn't," Newson admits. "I put wets on, he put dries on. My car was very quick at the start and I got the lead and thought I would never be caught, but the track dried, mine went off, and Stuart got very quick."

Newson also finished second in the British Championship to Paul Harrison, although this time the winner was never in doubt as Harrison streaked off round the first corner. Still, it was a good result considering that Newson was ill and his participation was in doubt at the start of the meeting.

Throughout the season, the lead in the grading points chart see-sawed between Newson and Tom Harris. Finishing top in the grading chart is an achievement which is not recognised by the governing bodies but which still carries kudos among fans and drivers alike, and it was the first time that Harris had a serious competitor for the honour. The stage was set for a rivalry which would smoulder for most of the season.

"That started on the Saturday night of the European Championship," Newson remembers. "The first heat was the Trust Fund race and I got put away really hard by Tom. From my point of view there was no reason why he wanted to do that, but he did. Then rumours got around that Tom had done it because I'm on the committee and we had a bit of a thing about his car. That really annoyed me. So I took it upon myself to make sure that he didn't win the European Championship. That's what I did and he went over the fence. That's what you did to me, so that's what I'm going to do to you now. Job done."

The yellow flags were waved to bring the race to a halt as Harris' wrecked car was removed from the track. Newson looked around and found himself in fourth position with four laps to go, still in with a chance of winning. The Wainman brothers and Speak got away at the start and Newson remained in position, crossing the line fourth, but was promoted to third after Rob Speak was disqualified for jumping the start.

"It didn't really bother me at all, I could have finished last." Newson explains. "Winning didn't matter. I did what I wanted to do."

Halfway through the season, the quest for the gold roof and the World Championship began to heat up. Newson finished third in the World Championship qualifying points, allowing him a front row start in one of the two World Semi-Finals.

"Even if I'd won the qualifying points I would have chosen the Stoke semifinal," Newson says. "Tom chose Skegness so it suited me. I was a bit worried about being outside front, but I was more worried about the track preparation. If it was going to be wet, the inside line would be good and the outside would

On the way to the World Final, winning the semi at Stoke...

be bad, but thankfully the track was in decent order so I had enough grip on the outside to get going."

Newson hoped that having clear air in front would help – for the past three years he had started on the second row and failed to progress to the World Final, the biggest race of the season.

"I had a bit of a game plan. I wanted to be first into the first corner and then go from there. It's one of those tracks where nobody can catch anybody, nobody can go quicker. It's bumpy. I knew that if I got out in front, I would be able to stay there just because they would struggle to catch me."

It worked out exactly as planned. Newson blasted down the straight and survived a kiss on his back bumper from pole sitter Frankie Wainman Junior. By the time he started the second lap, he had pulled a car length or two in the lead, safe from anything but the most suicidal of lunges.

"It's down to who dares go over the bumps quicker," Newson explains. "Stoke doesn't favour people who have really good equipment because it abuses it. I don't really enjoy racing there because of the way the track is, but I can see why the lower graders love it because it suits their old cars and style of racing."

The curse of Newson had been lifted. He had safely made it to the World Final, and he did it in emphatic style. Not everybody did. Reigning National Points Champion Ryan Harrison failed to complete the same race and was out of the

running for the gold roof, while Tom Harris did not progress through the other semi-final and had to implement the defending champion's right to start at the back of the World Final grid.

"From a fan's perspective it was a very boring race," Newson acknowledges, "but from where I was it was ideal! It was a textbook race. I got into the first corner first and Frankie didn't really give me too much bother. There was a little bit of action behind me which held them all up. I don't think anybody really rubbed me all race, I drove twenty laps and that was it."

When the World Championship grid was finalised after Paul Harrison won the second semi-final, a coin toss decided which of the two winners would start on pole position. Newson lost and was told he would be starting on the outside of the front row, the same position that he started the semi-final.

"Leading up to the World Final, a lot of people were asking me what my game plan would be, especially Paul Harrison! I kept telling everybody that I wanted Paul to go and I wanted to get behind him. But my game plan was exactly the same as the semi-final, I was going to hit the start and go! I did exactly what I wanted to do, I got a good start off the front and into the lead. But the trouble was that the reds came out on the first corner and they knew what I was going to do now! I gave my game away."

As it turned out, that wasn't a problem. Newson stuck to his guns and went with the same tactic that he had the first time round and in his semi-final – get to the first corner first. He did so and led the World Final for the first seven laps, but he couldn't create a gap as he had at Stoke.

"It wasn't meant to be. They told us at the pre-race briefing that they were going to water the track heavily to last the whole 25 lap race, so I set my car up so that it would do good at the start and hold on at the end. We went out on the parade lap and it was bone dry! After the first lap, when the reds came out, we had ten minutes to repair cars. I pulled onto the centre green – no damage – and my dad and I had an in-depth conversation. I said that we ought to change tyres and put dry tyres on. But I'd made such a good start that my dad thought we should stay as it was. We went on about it for so long, that the next thing they were telling us to line up and we still hadn't decided! Looking back I should have changed tyres, but hindsight is a wonderful thing. I survived a long time in front but I didn't have the speed in the dry conditions that I needed."

It was a tough call, but ultimately the decision not to change tyres was the wrong one.

"I put the tyres on that I should have in the Grand National and ended up winning easily. But all the drivers have their own 'if only' moment."

The destination of the gold roof had been decided. So had the black-and-white checks of the British Champion and the red-and-yellow checks of the European Champion. The only thing left to be decided was who would wear the silver roof. Newson led the National Points Championship Shootout from the off by virtue of his qualifying points and stayed in contention throughout, holding the lead going into eighth round at Birmingham. Then the sleeping rivalry with Tom Harris awoke in a fury.

"I got second in the consolation and was running fourth in the final when Tom put me away very hard again, a revenge hit for the Euro. That lost me a whole load of points and meant that going into the final round at Sheffield, we were all very close. It was the same thing again. Tom tried to stop me winning. I tried to stop Tom winning. Then it got to the Grand National, Tom and I were tied in the Shootout but he was also very close to me in the overall grading points. Losing the Shootout was one thing, but losing the grading points to Tom was another. I went out in the Grand National to make sure that Tom didn't score well and I didn't score well because of it. I won the grading points, Tom won nothing, which I was after."

There's an argument for saying that Newson sacrificed a real chance for silverware. As well as losing the Shootout, he also lost the Grand National Championship to Frankie Wainman Junior in that last race, all in order to secure a meaningless title, unrecognised by the sport, which carries no trophy or prize money.

Payback! Newson rolls Tom Harris in the European Championship

"Winning the grading points is pointless," Newson agrees, "but to know that I can beat Tom, Frankie or Rob Speak over a complete season showed me that I could do it. You can have one-off races and win the UK Open or British, but to outscore everybody over fifty meetings was a goal, I wanted to do it for myself. Whether I got anything for it or not was irrelevant."

What used to be the second most important title in the sport now no longer carries a title, trophy, prize or special roof colour. Many fans and drivers think that it should, Newson included.

"The Shootout is great for the fans," Newson admits. "It started because Frankie was the only driver doing all the meetings. When I was a nobody in the sport, Frankie had won the silver roof by World Final time. It was a one-way street. But now there are five or six drivers doing nearly every meeting. Danny and Frankie Wainman missed one, Tom Harris and Rob Speak only a missed handful. That's what made it close."

Ultimately, Newson ended the best season of his career with nothing to show for it.

"At the time I was happy. But when you get to the end of the year and look back – second there, second there, third in the Euro, won the semi, leading the World Final for so many laps, leading the Shootout – I realised I was so close. But it gives me something to aim for next year. I'm determined to do more and more and get better and better."

It's all well and good looking to the future, but does Newson look back on 2014 – the season where he came so close to glory on so many occasions – and wish that he had done things differently?

"I don't have regrets. I could regret not putting dry tyres on in the World Final, but in the UK Open, when I did switch tyres, Stuart beat me. You don't know how it would have worked out. I can look back and think I should have left Tom alone at Sheffield and gone for the Shootout, but at the time, that's what I was doing. That's just how it happened."

As another winter passes and a new season dawns again, Newson remains without a major championship title to his name. He is still ranked alongside Gaz Bott, Mick Noden and Bobby Burns – a good driver who hasn't managed to get on the top step of the podium when it counts the most.

"It will definitely come, it will happen," Newson says. "I'm desperate to win the World Final or the silver roof, of course. That's one of the things that keeps me going."

If he does win a major championship, there are certainly many in the sport who would be happy for him. There are those who have helped him get to where he is today, those who Newson himself has helped: anybody who has driven a Newson hire car, or whose cars have been fixed in the Newson garage, or who has driven a car built from scratch by him. And the Newson Racing Team would be ecstatic – a Newson win would make all the miles on the road and the attendance at every meeting worthwhile.

There's just one person who would be disappointed if Newson won a major championship. No, not Tom Harris; somebody closer to home.

"My daughter's favourite is Danny Wainman, he's her hero! She'd be gutted if I won and he didn't!"

The silver roof debate

Q: When is the top-scoring driver not the champion?
A: When he races a Formula 1 stock car.

The National Points Championship used to be a simple affair. The driver who scored the most points over a season was the winner and was entitled to wear silver to mark his achievement; initially two stripes, then from 1982 a completely silver roof.

The format wasn't perfect. It was a competition that could be dominated by one driver if they raced successfully over the vast majority of meetings. Stuart Smith Senior won thirteen consecutive titles between 1969 and 1981; Frankie Wainman Junior showed the same level of domination when he won seven in eight years up to 2001.

The National Series was introduced in 2002, a new format in which drivers raced for the silver roof over fewer meetings. The theory behind it was sound. It helped maintain interest towards the end of the season, encouraging crowds through the turnstiles. What was not sound was the management of the new competition. Constant tinkering and altering of the rules from season to season led to confusion among both spectators and drivers. The name of the championship was in constant flux too – the National Series, National Series Shootout, National Points Championship Shootout...

Why refuse to recognise the person who scores the most points over the season? The National Points Championship could still be won by the driver who scores the most points over the season, with the Shootout retained as a separate, discrete championship. An obvious solution would be to allow the person who scores the most points over the season to carry two silver stripes, just as they did prior to 1982. However, this would also force the governing bodies to recognise the official title and perhaps provide a little prize money. Maybe that's the reason why common sense does not prevail.

Whether the situation changes in the future or not, there's a substantial proportion of stock car fans who consider Mat Newson to be the real 2014 National Points Champion.

Theo van Lier

Motorsport is dangerous. Drivers are aware of and accept the risks every time they drive onto the racetrack. Deep down, they know that the danger is part of the thrill. Circling the track at speed with liberal use of the bumper means that accidents can, and will, happen. Ugly incidents like the one that occurred in the Netherlands on Sunday 17 August are a reminder that, when it goes wrong, serious injury and death can result.

It began as just another race – the second Formula 1 heat, a couple of hours after the World Cup race, a carnival atmosphere still present. Early on in the race, Danny van Wamelen sent Tom Harris wide with his bumper and overtook him. Harris got behind van Wamelen and pushed him wide at the end of the next straight, but the brunt of the force was passed onto Theo van Lier, a blue top who was in front of van Wamelen. The three cars were a runaway train charging into the corner.

Tyres smoked in a vain attempt to turn and both van Lier and van Wamelen hit the fence, but the biggest impact went through van Lier's 57 car. He was knocked unconscious, but either the throttle stuck or van Lier's foot depressed the pedal while he was out cold. The car scraped against the fence as it continued round the turn with nobody in control of it. As the track levelled out into the home straight, van Lier's car bounced back onto the racing line. It was twice hit by other cars speeding past, spinning and knocking it down the straight. It eventually came to rest but burst into flames.

Frankie Wainman Junior was the first off the mark. He ran from his position by the fence, where he was watching the race, and jumped onto the track. Rob Speak was the first of the drivers taking part in the race to react. He pulled up behind van Lier's car in an attempt to shield it and Wainman from oncoming traffic. After a few seconds, which must have seemed like a lifetime, the flames lowered enough to extricate van Lier from the cab. Alongside Wainman were Chris Cowley, Dylan Williams-Maynard, Ollie Ives, Lee Robinson, Wesley Schaap, Dan Johnson and Danny van Wamelen.

Van Lier's injuries were significant. Fractures were sustained to his leg, pelvis, spine, elbow and shoulder. Bruising to his brain was a concern, while the hot air he had inhaled caused further problems. His recovery has been slow and painful, but the fact that he has been able to make any recovery it all is due to the heroic efforts of the drivers and safety crew who risked their own lives to save van Lier's.

Yes, motorsport is dangerous, but so is all sport. Footballers have died of cardiac problems on the pitch. Cricketers have died after being hit by the ball. Rugby players have died after scrums collapsed. The risks have to be managed. Gone are the days when drivers circled the track in a rickety old car until it crumpled into

a fence, then ran to safety on the centre green while the race continued around them. Car design and construction has improved to prevent foreign objects infiltrating into the driver's cab. New procedures ensure that the race is temporarily halted if a driver requires aid or attention. HANS devices protect a driver's neck and spine, while fireproof clothing is compulsory.

The last UK fatality in Formula 1 stock cars occurred in 1995, when Johnny Goodhall was killed at Coventry. In the Netherlands, Piet Keijzer died at Venray ten years later. But a decade or two without a fatality is no reason for celebration. The work must not stop. If further reasonable measures can be taken to improve safety on the racetrack, they must be taken.

WORLD CUP CHAMPION

4

DAN JOHNSON

Like so many others, Dan Johnson is a second-generation stock car racing driver. His father, Dave, introduced Dan to the sport, lent his cars and taught Dan the basics. When Dan started to pick up a few good results, Dave hung up his own racing helmet and became Dan's crew chief and closest advisor, passing on his experience and guiding his son.

So when Johnson announced that he wanted to travel to the Netherlands to compete for the World Cup, the most prestigious prize in Dutch stock car racing, his father was the first to support him, right?

Wrong.

"My dad didn't want me to go," Johnson reveals. "He said that the car wouldn't be quick enough. But it made me try harder and prove him wrong. I spent a month working on the car, every night and weekend, changing lots of things to try to be quick over there. Obviously it paid off."

The odds were certainly packed against Johnson. It was his first time racing abroad and the tarmac track at Venray, in the southern Netherlands, was quite different to the British tarmac tracks with which Johnson was more familiar.

"Venray is a lot longer. That's mainly setup and checking the brakes, they need to be spot on. We put new calipers and new brake pads on, made sure the brakes were as good as we could get them. But what I spent a lot of time on was to make the car better in general, not just for Holland; things that I'd always wanted to try. It was a bit of a big gamble – the stuff that I did, it was either going work really well or fail miserably. Normally you would do one thing at a time and see how it changes things, but we did it all at once."

It was a huge gamble. These are finely tuned racing cars; the slightest change can have a big impact on performance. Coupled with Johnson's lack of experience at the longer Venray track, it was almost as though he was starting out as a white top again. Unfamiliar car, unfamiliar track.

"I went to practice at Northampton during the week before Venray and the car felt really good. We tried their tyres – the Dutch use a different inside rear tyre – and it still felt good. But when we went to Venray, Tom Harris nearly lapped me within about eight laps in the first practice session!"

I told you so: Johnson must have been expecting his father to say it. It looked like his dad was right – he wasn't going to be quick enough at Venray. The British drivers were about to compete in time trials to decide which of the slots they would take up on the grid.

"The car hadn't got enough stagger and there were a few other bits that needed improving, so we made some drastic changes again. Then the car just flew. Tom won the time trials and I was second. I think that shocked a lot of people. I wasn't far off his time. I wasn't bothered about the rest of that day's racing, I just wanted to qualify well for the World Cup. I was there to stop Tom and win."

Time trials were one thing. That was putting in fast, clean laps on an empty track. Winning the World Cup was another. Johnson was going to have to quickly adapt to the different racing style in the Netherlands.

"It's a lot faster," Johnson explains. "You have to respect each other over there because you can seriously hurt each other. If you hit people like you do around Northampton or Birmingham or any other track in Britain, then you will really hurt them. There is still contact, but it's much lighter."

It's a point that was emphatically underlined later that day when Dutch driver Theo van Lier suffered serious injuries. Johnson was one of the drivers who helped extricate an unconscious van Lier from his burning car.

Johnson's second-fastest time in the time trials put him on the outside of the third row for the World Cup race, to the side of the quickest Brit, defending champion and pre-race favourite, Tom Harris. In front of them were the four top Dutch qualifiers: Danny van Wamelen, Geert-Jan Keijzer, Lee Robinson (although English, registered as a Dutch driver) and Evert van der Berg. Behind them were another four Dutch drivers, then the next two fastest Brits in the time trials, Frankie Wainman Junior and Rob Speak.

"Tom wouldn't go at the start," Johnson remembers. "He was trying to hold me out wide because he was on the inside and I was on the outside. I think he thought I would try to destroy him right away. But as he was holding me out wide,

Ready to go in the World Cup – Johnson is the outside of the third row

Beginning to move through the field and towards the top three

About to overtake Geert-Jan Keijzer for second place – note Johnson's buckled rear wheel

Chequered flag and victory – second place is not even in sight

A little out of shape, but nothing that can't be rectified!

Johan Catsburg came up inside us. He was right behind Tom. So I put Catsburg into Tom and then I went on."

The impact meant that Harris suffered a flat tyre and was forced to retire. Johnson was in fourth place, but still with plenty of work to do. He ran wide after hitting Catsburg, which allowed Frankie Wainman Junior to gain on him going into the next corner. Just like Johnson snookered Catsburg into Harris, this time Wainman used Johnson to get at Danny van Wamelen. The impact knocked Johnson's car into the air and he clattered down with a bang. His outside rear wheel was buckled, but luckily the damage was not enough to slow him.

"I was probably nearly half a lap behind the leaders Lee Robinson and Geert-Jan Keijzer, so then I had to get pedalling! I was motoring and catching them up."

Johnson still had 29 of the 30 laps remaining – plenty of time yet. He slowly pulled back towards Wainman and by the halfway stage had him well within his sights.

"I think Frankie knew that I was miles quicker and let me go, which was quite good of him," Johnson says. That wouldn't have happened a couple of years before!

With half of the race still to run, Johnson had to catch and pass Keijzer and Robinson. He did. With a quarter of the race to run, Johnson was in the lead and passing backmarkers, giving him a cushion against a late surge. The longer the race

Winning the World Cup relieved some of the pressure on Johnson

went on, the quicker Johnson's car seemed compared to his opponents. By the time the chequered flag fell, he was the clear winner.

In standing on top of the podium in the Netherlands, Johnson joined a select group of British drivers. Brits first began to cross the Channel in the seventies to compete for the Long Track Championship at Baarlo. Once that circuit closed, British attention focused on the replacement World Cup at Venray. Peter Falding and Frankie Wainman Junior won multiple Dutch titles and Tom Harris recently started a period of British domination with back-to-back wins in 2012 and 2013. A successful invasion of the Netherlands is at risk of becoming an annual event. British drivers perform far better in the Dutch championships than the Dutch drivers do in the British ones. British drivers have won the flagship Dutch event multiple times, while the closest the Dutch have come to winning the World Championship is a second place by Dave Schaap in 2005.

"The Dutch aren't used to our aggression," Johnson suggests, "but more importantly, they lack on car setup. Lee Robinson should have been on the money to win. Geert-Jan Keijzer has the big fancy brakes and big engine. But I think that the British drivers are way in front on set up and altering the cars. All the Dutch come to the English to build their cars – no Dutch build them. But even if you have a pile of money and want the biggest engine, unless you have a driver who knows how to set it up, to alter it for a particular track or conditions, it's no good."

Going, going...

Johnson's World Cup drive saw him the clear winner: good car, great setup, perfect race strategy. It was a success which, strangely for a driver still towards the start of career, seemed to be a long time coming.

Johnson's racing career started young, although he initially flirted with other forms of oval racing – not one involving horsepower, but dogpower!

"My dad raced stock cars for over twenty years, but he was the first one in the family to do so," Johnson explains. "My grandad wasn't into cars. He was a dog man – greyhound racing. He wanted my dad to get into greyhound racing and he wanted me to as well. I was very close. We used go every Tuesday, Friday and Saturday. Grandad was a bit like stock car fans are – it didn't matter where in the country a greyhound meeting was, he would travel to it."

Once young Dan hit his teenage years, his father's fascination with motorsport began to win him over. Johnson started in Ministox but was soon driven out of that formula by the incessant politics and infighting between a few of the parents around at the time. The Johnsons bought a different kind of racing Mini and Dan raced in the junior grasstrack formula instead.

"I did pretty well in them," Johnson reveals. "Unlike Ministox, it was non-contact. But grasstracking taught me how to drive. You had to be smooth and you couldn't just hit people, you had to work your way around instead of just bashing then out of the way. Both Ministox and grasstrack help me now in Formula 1. If

I need to use my bumper, I will, but if I can be right with people and drive past them, I can as well."

After outgrowing the junior formulae, Johnson made the big step up to Formula 1 stock cars in 2006.

"I used my dad's car for the whole year on shale. It was a good learning curve. It was a big block, a big heavy car, so it didn't really matter. I also used my dad's tarmac car for a couple of months before I got my own. Dad raced up to my first year, then retired. He enjoyed it more watching me than racing himself. I raced a few times with him and he said, 'I was trying to watch where you were and what you were doing rather than concentrating on my own race!'"

Johnson didn't only have his father to pass on his wise words of experience. He could also turn to the person who had built cars for both Johnsons and who would be a key part of Team Johnson in Dan's early years – multiple World Champion, Peter Falding.

"Peter said not to hit anybody for at least a year. He told me to find my feet – a bit like Will Hunter has done. He's done well but he's been under the radar a bit. Next year he'll probably do a bit better. I did alright too, although I struggled with my tarmac car and the brakes. Peter couldn't get in it. He had made it small and low for me, so he couldn't see what was wrong. I struggled for about three months with the brakes and it turned out it was a dodgy master cylinder. So we changed that and that's when I started winning a few races."

The progression was steady. Johnson finished his first season as Novice of the Year under a blue roof. The following year he moved up to red and won the UK Open Championship. The season after, he made superstar for the first time and won the European Championship.

Then the momentum ground to a halt. 2009 saw just a solitary race win. The next four seasons saw Johnson taking the chequered flag regularly again, but never when it seemed to matter. He was always there or thereabouts: third place in the race for the silver roof in 2011, second place at the British Championship in the same year, two consecutive second places in the European Championship in 2012 and 2013. Yet Johnson never seemed to quite make it to the top step.

Above all, the close shaves that hurt the most were consecutive second places in the World Final in 2011 and 2012.

"I've been too close," Johnson admits. "In 2011 I did all the work. I took Frankie Wainman Junior out, took Tom Harris out, and I was leading for one lap, but Paul Harrison did the perfect hit and got me. At Skegness in 2012 I did all the work again. I took Tom out again and took a few others out of the reckoning but Lee Fairhurst just pipped me."

Some of the problem was that Johnson found himself drawing the attention of the other stars and superstars around him. It was partly a compliment – other drivers saw him as a threat, so they needed to stop him. It was also partly due to Johnson's own no-nonsense racing style which harks back to the older days of F1.

"Years ago, do you think Stuart Smith Senior used to care who was sponsoring him, who was building his car or if somebody had the same engine builder? Would he look at somebody else on track and think 'I'll be alright with him?' Did you ever see John Lund or Peter Falding have a go at each other after they'd been put in? It's the mentality of the drivers that has changed. There are a lot of cliques now. Some of the drivers dare not touch each other."

It's fair to say that Johnson hasn't been afraid to attack his opponents. A spat with Frankie Wainman Junior began at the end of the 2011 and continued into the next season. There have been numerous times the bumpers of the Johnson and Harris cars have hit each other hard – two drivers who came into the sport at about the same time, battling for supremacy.

Johnson is certainly aware of the near misses he has had in his quest for major championships. He makes no secret of the fact that missing out on titles in Britain is one reason why he went across the English Channel, against the advice of his father, to compete in the World Cup. It's part of the reason why he was prepared to gamble on car setup, rather than playing safe.

"I wanted to win so much in Holland. Once you've had a stint of winning, you want to win more and more. It's not a case of taking part, you want to win. You don't spend hours repairing the car and improving it to be average. With the pressure of my dad not wanting to go, I wanted to prove a point. And that's what I did. I wasn't confident that I was going to win, but I wanted it so much."

Johnson did win – but did it make up for missing out in the past?

"It relieved the pressure," Johnson admits. "I wouldn't say it was the same as winning the World Final, but there's still a lot of hype and there's not a lot of drivers who have gone over there and won it. It's definitely more of an achievement than winning the European Championship. How many English have won in Holland? And how many have tried to?"

Johnson isn't finished yet. The World Cup has put his career back on an upward trend, but his priority is still on winning the gold roof on British soil.

"It's got to come soon, I'm sure," Johnson says. "It's frustrating. I've been there or thereabouts but I haven't had the streak of luck. But there are still a lot of chaps who have been racing for a long time who haven't won it. A lot of people haven't got on the podium in a World Final. And I have."

Johnson v Wainman

The 2011 National Series Shootout went down to the wire, with three drivers having a mathematical chance of winning it in the last race. Dan Johnson was the third of three, although his was the toughest task. He effectively needed to win the race, with Frankie Wainman Junior and Craig Finnikin failing to finish, to take the silver roof for the following year.

Johnson was well aware what he needed to do – and boy, did he try to do it. As soon as the green flag dropped, Johnson drove Wainman into the Belle Vue fence. There was no chance Wainman would finish the race. But Finnikin got away, his sixth place more than he needed to take the title. Johnson's fifth place saw him finish a single point behind Wainman in the final standings.

"Frankie had put me in earlier in the Shootout at Northampton when Lee Fairhurst wrecked his tarmac car," Dan explains. "He put about four or five of us in, he stacked us all in a little pile, you couldn't have done it with a forklift. It was a good hit but I was really miffed off. That's why I cost him the silver roof, really. I still had a chance of winning it too, so I tried to put him in and go and win it. Frankie had cost me so much money in damage in his attempt to win the silver roof, so I was going to do the same to him to try and win the silver roof."

515

Frankie Wainman Jnr.

Silsden - West Yorkshire

And suddenly a new rivalry was born. Wainman has had his fair share over the years, now Johnson was added to the list.

"Payback's a bitch, especially as hard as that one will be," Wainman declared. "Stock car drivers have got good memories. Especially this one."

"Then it was getting a bit ridiculous," Johnson says. "We were taking each other out in heats for nothing important. It carried on for about four or five months. In the end I said to Frankie, 'do you want to carry on or do you want to call it quits? All we're doing is taking each other out and the rest are winning.' Now we're friends and I can race him fair."

Whether the ceasefire survives next time Wainman and Johnson in a close fight for a title remains to be seen!

WORLD CHAMPION
55
CRAIG FINNIKIN

"Gentlemen, start your engines!"

Flags wave as 36 V8 engines roar into life. 'Fanfare for the Common Man' plays over the tannoy as the best stock car drivers in the world slowly edge around the shale racetrack on two rolling laps. The next few minutes will decide the Formula 1 Stock Car World Championship.

The atmosphere is tense, rippling with anticipation. Goosebumps rise on the flesh of the watching fans. Pulses race amongst the drivers inside the cars.

Paul Harrison is in unfamiliar territory. He is starting his 26th World Final, but only the first from pole position. Beside him is Mat Newson, winner of the other World Semi-Final. Both have tried to plan a strategy for the biggest race of the season. Newson has been telling anybody who will listen that he will tuck in behind Harrison and go into the first corner in second place. In reality, he intends to do nothing of the sort. He wants to get a quick start and take the first corner in the lead. Harrison's strategy is simpler. Survival. After working all season to get on the World Final grid, he doesn't want it to end on the first corner. It's a fifty-bend race. He'll be happy to exit the first corner in the top five.

When the green flag falls, Newson races away and succeeds in getting round the corner in first place. Harrison follows. Then the carnage begins. A push from Frankie Wainman Junior from the fourth row sends the top Dutch qualifier, Koen Maris, into Dan Johnson. He glances off his fellow second row starter, Rob Speak. Johnson is fortunate, the nudge swivelling him into the turn at a good angle. Speak is less fortunate. He goes the other way, head on into the fence.

The rest of the field follows in. After a few seconds, half the cars are stuck in the melee. Bumpers hook onto bumpers, tyres stick on nerf rails. With cars trapped and the track blocked, the starter waves the red flag and signals a complete restart.

Five cars fail to make the restart, including Speak and both Dutch qualifiers on the third row, leaving gaps towards the front of the grid. Newson had played his hand early. What would he do now? Exactly the same. He leads into the first turn for a second time when the green flag waves again, Harrison goes through in second, but Dan Johnson does enough to force him wide at the end of the back straight: Johnson into second, Frankie Wainman Junior into third. Harrison immediately counter-attacks and retakes third on the first corner of the second lap before a rolled car forces waved yellow flags and a temporary halt to the race.

This time, the restart sees the cars in single file. Newson has more breathing room but is aware of the bumper of Johnson nudging him on the rolling lap. He keeps the lead under pressure, but Harrison begins to fall down the order. His car needs a little time to bed in and he doesn't have that luxury in the frantic first laps of the World Final. Just as the field is beginning to stretch and things seem to be calming down, American Eric Pollard spectacularly rolls and his car comes to rest against the fence. Yellow flags again. Six laps down, another restart.

Johnson taps the back bumper of Newson again on the rolling lap. He is impatient. Two laps later, Johnson takes the lead, but Newson is not out of it yet. He counters, first sending Johnson out wide but not enough to retake first place, then mistimes and spins himself. Disaster! Newson is relegated to seventh place and Johnson sails off down the back straight, unchallenged.

Johnson continues to circle the shale oval with a healthy lead. He drives carefully, within himself, saving the car, wary of backmarkers. The engine is a little hot – hotter than he would like – so he doesn't dip the throttle quite as much as he could. For eleven laps, Johnson leads the World Championship. It looks like he is going to win. After consecutive second places in 2011 and 2012, he will finally earn the right to bear the gold roof.

The first lap board is shown by the starter, indicating five laps to go. Johnson leads, but coming up fast is car number 55. Craig Finnikin. Where did he come from?

"I'd liked to have started a bit further forward," Finnikin reveals, "but I wasn't too worried because at Coventry it always seems that you get that big first bend, a few hits and a big pile up. And it happened! I got stuck on the outside and couldn't get across to the inside. I could see that everybody on the inside was pushing so I stuck it right against the fence and slowed down as much as I could. I ended up getting caught at the tail end of the pile up but luckily the race was red flagged. I got out alright with no damage and it wiped a few of the top drivers out. On the second restart I managed to get onto the inside and survived a few hits in the first few laps."

Finnikin's strategy was similar to Paul Harrison's: just survive the first few laps. Being on the outside of the eighth row meant that he couldn't really plan for the first corner – it was a case of rolling the dice and seeing how they fell. His luck was good. The yellow flags also aided his cause, briefly suspending the race, closing the gaps and preventing the front runners from getting away. After the first yellow flag on the second lap, Finnikin had moved from the sixteenth starter to tenth place. After the second yellow flag, on lap six, he was up to eighth.

"I kept picking other cars off. I got away clean on the last restart; the track slicked up and came good for me. I didn't push for two or three laps, so just before halfway I was sixth or seventh. I saved the car until the second half of the race because I knew that around Coventry the car always comes good. I decided to start pushing from there. I kept reeling them in and picking them off and the car got faster as the race went on – or everybody else got slower!"

There's no doubt about it – Finnikin was in the fastest car on track. The gap between him and the leader noticeably narrowed after he overtook Mick Sworder for second place. At first, it was a case of *could* he catch Johnson before the chequered flag. It quickly became a matter of *when*.

"I could tell that I was catching him hand over fist," Finnikin remembers. "I hit Dan hard going into the first turn with five laps to go but I thought it was nowhere near good enough, so I slowed down and let him come back past me. Then I hit him going into the turn at the end of the back straight which sent him right out to the fence. I wanted to get rid of him far enough to get a gap because if I didn't he'd be back on me on the next bend. As luck has it there was a parked car there – but I didn't know that! I was more focused on getting through the traffic and catching Dan because he had a good lead."

It was a perfectly timed hit, regardless of whether or not there was good luck involved when Johnson hit the retired car. Johnson remained in the race but his progress was delayed and he had no chance of retaliating. Finnikin was left with four laps between him and his first World Championship title.

"It seemed like the longest four laps ever! I was watching backmarkers. I was listening for rattles and vibrations on the car. When I caught backmarkers I slowed right down to make sure that none of them popped a tyre, which is quite easily done. I just made sure I finished."

The chequered flag waved, the fireworks erupted. For the first time in his career, Finnikin would be able to race under the gold roof of the World Champion.

"It's the main thing we race for all year," Finnikin says. "It's very important. Especially since my dad won it as well. To have another Finnikin name on the trophy is unbelievable."

Paul Harrison enjoyed the benefits of pole position in the 2014 World Final

But Rob Speak didn't enjoy the view at the end of the home straight on the first lap

More and more joined Speak and the first start turned into carnage

Dan Johnson looked quick once they were going again

New Zealander Peter
Bengston was the first of
two international drivers
to roll over

Mat Newson led them
away on both restarts, but
keep an eye out for Craig
Finnikin, two cars behind
Harrison's chequered roof

Once he hit the
front, Finnikin was
uncatchable

And pretty happy to
capture the biggest title
of his career!

Helping Dad celebrate his World Final win – this time he was allowed to the track!

Finnikin's journey to the gold roof started early. Stock car racing is in the Finnikin blood. His grandfather, Charlie, raced as early as 1955 – only Paul Harrison can claim a longer lineage in the sport. Charlie raced until his death from a heart attack in 1973, by which point his son Bert had also started behind the wheel. Bert took over his father's number 55 and raced under it for the next 25 years, the highlight of which was winning the World Championship at Odsal in 1990.

"I don't remember Dad winning the World Final, I was only nine years old," Craig says, "although I've seen the video plenty of times. I didn't actually go to Odsal, apparently I'd been naughty! We got a phone call saying that he'd won. I thought he was winding us up, I didn't believe him until he came home with the trophy. The trophy was that big that I sat in it when he got back."

Young Craig's behaviour didn't stop him from being given the opportunity to race in junior formulae when he became old enough. A few appearances at nearby Stoke in Formula Fiat were followed by an eighteen-month stint in Ministox. After that, he joined Formula 2 alongside his father, who had made the move from F1 at the end of the nineties. Bert was one of the top F2 drivers – perhaps the best not to have won the gold or silver roof in the formula – and Craig soon joined him, becoming a red top in his second season. Cousin Stuart also raced Formula

Finnikin tries a little off-roading at Knockhill early in his career

2, but transferred to Formula 1 for the new millennium. It was a move which did not interest Craig – until he drove one.

"I raced a Formula 1 when I was 21. My cousin let me race his car at Coventry. After racing that I put all my Formula 2 stuff up for sale and started to build a Formula 1. It didn't really interest me until I had a go in one – and that was it! I built my own car and Dad bought my first engine. I think I've probably built about ten cars since."

Finnikin made a conscious decision, like that of Stuart Smith Junior, not to rely on other car builders. Right from the start, he built his own cars from the ground up.

"Everything I've raced in Formula 1 I've built myself. I built one for Lenny Smith and one for Shaun Blakemore too, but when I've finished work and done my own car I haven't really got time for others."

The family business, a HGV workshop, gave Finnikin the mechanical experience and equipment he needed to construct and maintain his stock cars. It also gave him the freedom to experiment and try different things. This was most noticeable in the tilter car, debuted in 2011. The tilted tarmac car slanted to the side in an attempt to improve weight distribution and cornering speed. It was a radical design – probably the most radical of the past decade – but ultimately it did not bring success and only lasted a few meetings.

A radical new look – the tilter

"I keep saying I'm going to rebuild it!" Finnikin jokes. "It was probably one of the quickest cars I've built in timescale, it just seemed to work out as I wanted it, but there was a hoo-hah on how the engine was mounted. I had the scrutineers check it out. The rules used to state that the centre line of the engine had to be in the drop of the chassis, but with the chassis rails being on an angle it offset the engine even more and the engine was leaning over as well. If it had won everything they'd have wanted to ban it – which was a reason to not keep going with it. I also decided I wanted to alter the suspension and stuff, and with how the chassis was I couldn't do what I wanted, so I had to build a new one. They've altered the rules a lot so I probably wouldn't be able to use it now. But if you don't try something, you won't get anywhere."

The tilter joins John Lund's short wheelbase, Chris Elwell's space frame, Andy Smith's stepped chassis and John Stirk's six-wheeler as one of the iconic cars in stock car history. Not all were successful, but all dared to be different. The tilter is still at the Finnikin workshop, slowly rusting. Perhaps it will make a comeback some day. Experimentation is, after all, a good thing.

"I experiment all the time. To most people the cars look the same but they're not! All year you try different stuff and try find that little bit of edge – different tyre pressures, moving axles about a little bit. Most people design it on paper, I just design it as I go along. If it doesn't work, just chop it off and move it!"

And something more conventional – the one that won the World Final

As well as developing new cars, Finnikin has also developed his driving style. Three of Finnikin's first four meeting final wins came on tarmac. But since then, every meeting final he has won – 21 up until the end of the 2014 season – has been on shale. Always a regular on the loose stuff, he picked up the subtle differences in technique and has developed a reputation as something of a specialist. If Tom Harris is the man to beat on tarmac, Finnikin is the man to beat on shale.

"Shale is a lot easier than tarmac," Finnikin says. "I think driving style is a little bit more important. On tarmac you have to have your car spot on and everything has to be smooth."

Considering Finnikin's obvious talent for shale racing, here's a fact that you might find interesting: it wasn't until July 2012, when Finnikin won the British Championship, that he won a meeting final at Coventry. Then he won three on the trot, another two in 2013, and one in 2014 – along with the World Final, of course.

"It just clicked. Messing about with the car and finding a better setup and changing my driving style seemed to work. I've gained experience and maybe had a bit of luck as well. You do need a bit of luck. But I've learned to sit and wait and not get involved in the fight and pick them off afterwards. If you get into a battle you go backwards, unless you can get a good hit and get them out of the way so they can't hit you."

Silver roof, National Points Champion

The British Championship that marked Finnikin's first final victory at Coventry wasn't his first major success. That came in the Shootout in 2011, when he entered the finale at Belle Vue in third place, having fought back from seventh place in the standings after four rounds.

Winning the Belle Vue final meant that Finnikin needed to place in the Grand National and hope that Frankie Wainman Junior did not finish well. Finnikin was helped by an outside contender, Dan Johnson, who planted Wainman into the wires as the green flag fell. Finnikin was left to circle the track and ensure he finished – a strategy which he thinks is the best way to win the silver roof.

"Keep out of the way and keep scoring points," Finnikin says. "The silver roof is probably a bigger challenge to win than the World Final. We do it over ten rounds, but you also have to qualify for it. But the World Final is the one that you get most recognised for."

And it was the one that was missing from Finnikin's trophy cabinet at the start of the 2014 season. He had stood on the World Championship podium – second in 2013, third in 2010 – but he never stood a realistic chance of winning. In 2013, Tom Harris was way ahead and cruised to victory. In 2010, Finnikin had worked his way through from the tenth row but to overhaul Andy Smith from there was asking too much.

Gold roof, World Champion

Finnikin's eyes were firmly focused on winning the World Final. A new shale car was unveiled at the start of the season with the biggest race of the season in mind. But the plan started to unravel slightly with a sixth-place finish in his Skegness semi-final after trading bumper paint with Mick Sworder and Paul Hines. Finnikin would have to start the World Final on the outside of the eighth row. It was going to take a great drive and expert preparation if he was going to make the podium again.

"We played around with the new shale car a few times at Coventry this year," Finnikin says, "but I was struggling with the brakes. It was good first time out and alright second time, but the third time it just seemed to have gone backwards. It was in the back of my head to try the old car again so at the last minute I took it to the meeting at Coventry a couple of weeks before the World Final. I was happier with it, I've always been comfy in it, it's as soft as anything and although it was six years old it felt alright. I decided to race it at the World Final and tweaked the settings all night. During the next week I scaled it, measured it up and messed about with it. It paid off!"

The decision to use that car helped Craig Finnikin to write his name into the history books. The Finnikin name was already one which was inextricably linked to Formula 1 stock cars. Now the family boast the first third-generation racer to become World Champion.

Great World Finals

Three long-time leaders, two rollovers, one brilliant hit. The 2014 World Final will go down in the archives as one of the best, joining these classic World Finals...

1972: A terrific battle between Stuart Smith and Doug Cronshaw ended with Smith in the lead going into the final lap. Willie Harrison made an all-or-nothing dive on the last bend, but he ended up with nothing, while Smith had his second gold roof.

1984: Len Wolfenden looked poised to take his second World Final after second-placed Dave Mellor held out against Stuart Smith for seventeen laps. But Smith's brilliance shone through and he eventually made his way past both for his fifth world title.

1991: Peter Falding launched a last bender on Bert Finnikin and it looked like he would take the title, but Richard Pratt's intervention from a lap down stopped him. John Lund sneaked through the carnage to take the win. A more spectacular half lap has never been seen.

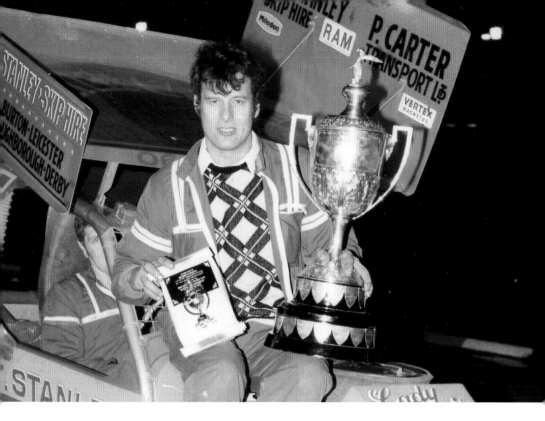

1995: John Lund took the lead from Frankie Wainman Junior. Andy Smith took the lead from John Lund. Keith Chambers took the lead from Andy Smith. And that's the way it stayed, despite Chambers being pressured by Peter Falding for half the race.

1999: A remarkable last five laps in which Andy Smith and Frankie Wainman Junior battled for the lead before John Lund came along to try and take them both out. The result? All three hit the fence and Murray Harrison sneaked by for an unexpected win.

2012: Only on the grid as a reserve – courtesy of his own father's withdrawal – Lee Fairhurst made the most of the big hits on the first corner and moved through the field to take the chequered flag, despite starting in last place.

And finally... 1990: By the second half of the race, Finnikin was visibly catching the leader and made his way past for a deserved victory. Sound familiar? This time it was Bert Finnikin overtaking John Lund at Odsal for the first Finnikin World Championship.

NATIONAL POINTS CHAMPION
318
ROB SPEAK

Is Rob Speak the best racing driver in the history of oval motorsport?

It's a difficult question to answer, but Speak did his credentials no harm at all when he captured the final championship of the sixtieth F1 stock car season, the second most prestigious of the sport: the National Points Championship. In doing so, Speak wrote his name in the record books yet again – the only driver to have won gold and silver roof in both Formula 1 and Formula 2 stock cars.

Speak's time in Formula 1 only began after he had spent a decade in Formula 2 stock cars, a period that saw such domination that it is never likely to be repeated in any formula. He won the National Points Championship eleven times in succession, including as a raw seventeen-year-old in his first full season. He won eight World Championships, including six in succession between 1994 and 1999. Put simply, Speak was unstoppable behind the wheel of his F2.

Unstoppable on the track, at least. Speak's reign in Formula 2 came to an end at the end of nineties due to off-the-track disputes. Promoters tried to refuse him bookings, disciplinary sanctions curtailed his racing. Speak felt like he was being pushed out of the sport. In truth, Formula 2 was getting a bit fed up of Rob Speak. But Rob Speak was getting a bit fed up with Formula 2 as well.

"It had run its course and I wasn't enjoying it any more," Speak reveals. "I decided that I would pack it in and go banger racing for a bit."

It would have been a shame for a talent such as Speak's to be lost to bangers. It didn't take long for the Formula 1 world to rally round and persuade him to give the big league a try. Among those who wanted to tempt Speak was Jamie David-son, a red top driver based in the Greater Manchester area like Speak.

"I borrowed Jamie's car for a couple of meetings, enjoyed it and did well so I went down the road of Formula 1; just went into it."

Speak had been hoping to get away from the controversy and friction in F2 and have a bit of fun in the bangers, where nobody takes racing too seriously and nothing can't be fixed with a sledgehammer and a blowtorch. Now he was moving up into the premier formula in UK oval racing.

"It was a hard six months," Speak reveals. "I had lots of feuds – let's put it that way! Straight away, it was instant. To come out of Formula 2 into Formula 1 was a bit of an intimidating jump. They're bigger, they're harder, but I didn't want to be pushed around. I was the top in my sport."

Speak may have won everything there was to win in Formula 2 – multiple times – but as far as most F1 drivers were concerned, he had just been the big fish in a small pond. Now he was with the sharks.

"At the start, everybody was chopping my nose off every time I passed them. They were trying to say, 'you're not coming into my job.' So I went out with the intention of roughing it up a bit with Andy Smith and Frankie Wainman Junior. None of us wanted to back down. One of them was wrecking me every week or I was wrecking them. And then, six months in, they realised and all the other driv-ers realised that I was here to stay. I'd earned their respect. I think it was good for the sport, for the spectators."

In his second full season, the first of the new millennium, Speak debuted a new tarmac car at the European Championship. It had been built by his arch-rival on the track, Frankie Wainman Junior.

"Frankie had a brand new car as well that day. It was quite a sensible meeting for once because Frankie and I both had new cars and we didn't want to wreck them. Come the European Championship race, Frankie got second and I won it. But I think that if I hadn't got a new Wainman car, he would have wrecked me – we were bumper to bumper for a lot of the time."

The following year, Speak returned to Northampton to defend his title.

"I was in Jamie Davidson's old car again by then. He'd packed in and had given it to me. That year it was the dominant car, especially round Northampton. The European Championship race was quite easy. No dramas, just nice and steady, which is what you need when you have the quickest car."

Having retained the title, Speak started to push for bigger honours. Only Dave Chisholm had managed to win the gold roof in both Formula 1 and Formula 2, and Speak had his eye on history, as well as his biggest rival.

"I was battling with Frankie again by that point," Speak says. "At the Buxton semi-final I could have passed Frankie, but I decided to sit behind him for sec-

Speak finds an unorthodox way of dealing with Frankie Wainman Junior

ond because it was a better position for the World Final. Andy Smith had won his semi-final, Frankie had won his semi-final, so that put me, I thought, in the dominant position behind them on the second row. I went out for pre-World Final practice and only did about five laps. My team thought that something was wrong, but the car felt good, everything felt brilliant. So I did about five laps, put a heat cycle through the tyres, pulled on the centre green and parked up. We never touched it after that."

Speak knew he was driving the best car and was confident in his own ability. He knew that the race was his for the taking.

"Everybody thought that I was going to go in with a big one and wreck them, but I didn't need to. They both wrecked each other and I drove up the inside. There was a yellow flag and restart, by this time both Andy and Frankie were damaged. I just sat back, they both wrecked each other again, and I drove up the inside and away. It was an easy race."

Speak might have fallen into Formula 1 by accident, but he had proven himself to be one of the best cross-formula racers, one of two to have won the gold roof in both F1 and F2. The following year, Speak came close to defending the title and earning his tenth World Championship crown, but John Lund knocked him off the top step.

The newest rival – Speak and Moodie take each other out of the F2 World Final

Yet by now, the novelty had worn off and Formula 1 was beginning to vex Speak as much as Formula 2 did. His exit from F1 came with a bang – literally – at Wimbledon in October 2002. It is a meeting which will be remembered as one of the most remarkable in the history of the sport.

"Yes, Wimbledon," says Speak with a wry smile. "I'd had enough by that point. I always said that I'd pack in around the time that I was thirty. All I'd known was racing. At some point you either have to accept that that's your life or you want something better. And that's what I decided to do – I'd buy a farm and do some work with horses."

So what does Speak remember about his final meeting?

"I remember that there was plenty of hassle! Me and Wainman had raced the night before and we'd had a bit of hassle there. In the heat we were racing, no problem, and then in the final he stuck me in hard. I was a bit annoyed about it because all meeting we'd been bumper to bumper and he'd waited until the final to bury me. So we fixed the car. We rushed about to mend it for the Grand National but it had no brakes, we didn't have time to fix the pipes up. The scrutineers were saying that I couldn't race but I ignored them and drove onto the back. I knew that I didn't need brakes for what I was going to do!"

Wainman was in a tough fight with Andy Smith for the new National Series Championship and made the mistake of passing Speak with a small tap, leaving

Speak lurking ominously behind. The following bend, both Wainman and Speak found themselves lodged in the wires after Speak's kamikaze attack. Wainman faced a struggle to get his car fixed for the end of the season, but Speak had no intention of fixing his. Goodbye Formula 1.

After a year or two of non-contact ASCAR racing, during which time Speak briefly teamed up with Ben Collins (alias The Stig on *Top Gear)*, Speak walked away from motorsport completely. For six years he had little to do with oval racing beyond an occasional appearance in a banger. Then the lure of competitive racing and the chance to help out a few old buddies became too much to resist. It was Terry George, Speak's former car constructor, who first got him back into Formula 2 in 2009.

"Terry was building a car and asked if I would try it out for a couple of meetings," Speak says. "He hadn't built a Formula 2 for a long time and wanted to try to get back into it. He wanted to get some interest in his business. The car wasn't going that well so I tried to do more and more meetings until it got sorted. But I wouldn't say I have done any good in Formula 2 until I started to race on shale again. I wanted a good shale car for a one-off meeting. Darren Bingley had hurt his back so I asked if I could race his car and he said no problem. Darren then said that I could race it at a few more meetings. It was exactly the situation as Jamie Davidson in Formula 1 all those years ago. I didn't intend to race but it picked up momentum and kept going. You do alright and then somebody asks you to do another meeting."

Speak's occasional appearances were enough for him to qualify for a F2 World Championship Semi-Final in 2009, one of the first times he came up against a new rival: Gordon Moodie. Speak has had many rivalries over the years: Les Palmer, Bill Batten, Andy Smith and Frankie Wainman Junior are names that spring to mind. Yet the ongoing battle with Moodie would become the fiercest conflict of his career.

Moodie was the new dominant force in Formula 2. At the stage they met, he had won the National Points Championship five times and had only lost the title after a controversial ban denied him the World Final crown and prevented him winning the silver roof in 2008 and 2009. No doubt Moodie saw a returning Speak as a threat, while Speak wanted to show the young pretender that the old master still had it in him. Moodie was a smooth driver, akin to a hot rodder, while Speak was happy to use the bumper. England v Scotland, old hand v young gun, bumper v speed – everything seemed to clash.

The spat first surfaced in 2011 at the World Championship Semi-Finals at Hednesford. Speak held the lead and Moodie sat behind him, refusing to pass, even when Speak slowed to give him a chance. It was a strategy with which Speak took umbrage. Moodie had refused to rise to the challenge.

"He settled for second and I couldn't understand it," Speak says. "He was so much faster than me. He should have eliminated me out of the World Final. That's what annoyed me."

Wait a second – didn't Speak do exactly the same thing earlier in his career? Didn't he wait behind Frankie Wainman Junior so he could start the F1 World Final on the second row?

"It was a different scenario!" Speak laughs. "To pass Wainman, I would have had to take him out. I couldn't have got past him without wrecking him, and I'd probably have gone in with him, and neither of us would have finished. But Moodie settled behind me when he could have passed me clearly and driven away from me. He should have buried me that day. If you're both on the pace, it's very difficult to bury somebody, but when somebody is much slower, it's so easy to bury them. He would have won the World Final that year. If it had been the other way round, I'd have made sure that he wasn't in it."

Speak let everybody know that he was unhappy, but a monsoon on the rolling lap of the World Final turned the King's Lynn shale into a quagmire and he had no chance to express his dissatisfaction with Moodie on the track. Perhaps Moodie listened to the criticism, because at the following year's semi-final he tried (and failed) to take out Speak with a lap to go. The rivalry simmered until the 2013 World Final at Taunton, when Speak and Moodie knocked lumps out of each other. They were fighting for the lead, but more importantly it seemed, they were each fighting to make sure that the other did not win. The result? Neither finished the race. A bad-tempered exchange at Bill Batten's testimonial meeting at the same track the following season focused the build up to the next World Final on Speak and Moodie once again. Speak qualified on the inside of the second row, a strong position to challenge for the gold roof, but his priorities lay elsewhere. When he found Moodie behind him after three laps, hoping to take third position, Speak sat on his brakes. Moodie was held back for more than half a lap, allowing cars to stream past.

Has the rivalry with Moodie spoiled Speak's return to Formula 2?

"It's just the World Final," Speak says. "I've said that many times. If I'm in it, he won't win and I won't win. If I can qualify for the World Final, that's all I'm bothered about."

If Speak's comeback in Formula 2 has seen him court controversy, his comeback to Formula 1 has been the opposite. It started, like before, with a favour.

"That's how all my racing has been – I don't intend to do any, then I get a phone call! It wasn't my intention to go back into Formula 1, I thought that was finished. Then a promoter phoned me up and asked if I would race a charity meeting in Formula 1. But he knew what he was doing! It was a World Championship qualifying round and I got a place in a semi-final. I didn't want to do the semi-

final but people were asking me to. I ended up doing the semi and qualifying for the World Final. Before I knew where I was, I was back racing again."

The 2013 season saw Speak back in action in an F1, combining his time with F2, racing mainly on tarmac in the bigger formula. Then Formula 1 became the priority in 2014, with a car for each surface. The old team of Speak and Jamie Davidson was reunited, with Stephen Sayers – known to all as Cecil – as chief spanner.

"I do as I'm told!" Speak jokes. "Jamie is 100% in charge and Cecil runs the full package of the cars, from when they get unloaded to when they get loaded up again. I go over occasionally on Fridays to help out with the tyres and one thing and another, but Cecil is kept busy. Jamie organises everything else. I think he just likes the way I drive. He loves the sport and he loves it when I'm racing. I'm lucky that people are interested in the racing that I do, and we're good friends off the track."

Speak started the 2014 season like a greyhound out of the trap. Three consecutive meeting finals wins, together with five heat wins over seven meetings and a Grand National victory thrown in for good measure, meant that he earned the flashing lights of a superstar for the first time since his return.

"It just clicked," Speak says. "The tyres that we went on to suited me. They have a lot less grip; you have to drive it a little bit differently. There's no instant

Leading the pack

power when you come out of the corner, you've got to feed it in and control it a little bit more. It suited me better. And we went on to one shocker. It slowed the pace down and it was easier to shove people wide and get past them. It suited my style of driving."

Perhaps Speak also benefited because there wasn't an F1 equivalent of Gordon Moodie – somebody who was prepared to put his body and bumper on the line to stop him. The old rivalry with Frankie Wainman Junior had dissolved during Speak's time away, to be replaced by a grudging respect for each other. Tom Harris didn't see the need to single him out, nor did Mat Newson. Has it been easier to race a Formula 1 this time round because of that?

"The first time," Speak says, "the rumours were going round the pits. 'Rob Speak is coming to Formula 1, will he be any good?' 'He won't do any good in our formula, we'll show him!' The second time, I didn't need to prove myself. It's not as aggressive now."

Speak qualified for the Shootout – the third-highest scorer of the twelve who made the cut – and progressed through the initial rounds relatively unnoticed, slipping under the radar. Not the kind of racing strategy usually associated with Rob Speak: softly, softly, catchee monkey.

Yet keep an eye on Speak at the start of a race. He may have a reputation for throwing his front bumper at whoever is in front of him, but more often than not, he'll pass a handful of opponents without touching them. He seems to have the ability to find a gap and slip through it effortlessly. A finer driver on the first lap you won't find on the track, and another sign that Speak is a master of his craft – not simply a hard hitter.

Speak was helped in his quest for the silver roof by the fact that Stuart Smith Junior just missed out on qualifying for the Shootout. Starting in front of the Shootout drivers, Smith was able to get away and was simply uncatchable. Of the four Shootout rounds that Smith contested, he won five races. Those were points that would have been a valuable addition to somebody else's tally, most notably the meeting final at Coventry which denied Frankie Wainman Junior the chequered flag.

With Smith hoovering up points, it was Speak's consistency which won him the Shootout. He finished 29 races during the Shootout rounds, more than any other, each position adding points to his total. Of his closest rivals, Tom Harris finished 24, Mat Newson 26, Frankie Wainman Junior 25.

With no one driver building up a lead, at what point did Speak realise that the silver roof was his for the taking?

"I knew that I was in with a shout at King's Lynn, the fourth round of the Shootout. I was winning the final when I got a puncture, but the car just seemed to have clicked. We knew what we had to adjust to make it do what we wanted. If I'd won that race I would have been in a great position. As it was, the halfway point was after the meeting at Skegness. I was really trying to get into the top six, because if you're not in the top six by that point I don't think you have a chance, plus you get more start money. Then winning the final in the seventh round at King's Lynn got me up to about fourth. At that stage I decided I was going to really go for it. I wasn't going to lose by not trying."

Going into the Shootout finale at Sheffield, Speak sat atop the table on 281 points. The double points on offer meant that five others were still in with a chance: Mat Newson, Tom Harris, Craig Finnikin, Danny Wainman and Frankie Wainman Junior. Yet Speak was a strong favourite.

Sheffield is not the ideal venue to deliver a nail-biting end to the competition. Never a particularly popular venue in terms of driver attendance, Speak was well aware that all he needed to do was circulate safely, wait for lower-grade drivers to make mistakes, and pick up places. Like the rest of the Shootout, consistency was the key. Not that Speak would admit to that.

"I just took it like a normal meeting," Speak says. "I wanted to win. I didn't drive conservatively."

Only when Mick Sworder appeared behind Speak in the first heat and Craig Finnikin nibbled at Speak's bumper in the meeting final did it ever look like he might be in trouble, but both incidents were resolved without Speak breaking sweat.

"Mick is a hard driver but I didn't think he would take me out because he wasn't in with a chance," Speak explains. "Finn had a go at me and was about the only person that did. He tried to put me in the top corner but was a little bit unsure coming down the inside of me. I managed to put him in the fence and that eliminated him! I think that was the only close point during the meeting."

Two third-places, a fifth and a sixth were enough – indeed, the eleven-point lead he had at the start of the day stretched to 25 points by the end. Perhaps the only disappointment was that Speak wasn't tested. He'd rather have lost the title but been involved in a good scrap rather than winning it at a canter.

"Mat Newson is a good driver, a fast driver, but he didn't go for it," Speak says. "To win something like that you've got to go for it, you can't sit back and wait for somebody to make a mistake. You just need to get going, don't you? Tom Harris didn't deal with me at all. He could have done. I was behind him and thought that I had to pass him. I passed him, he got back, and then I passed him again. He should have dealt with me."

It's a trait of the newer style of drivers that Speak has noticed since his second spell in Formula 1 started.

"Tom Harris would have won this year's World Semi-Final at Skegness. But I wanted to win it too. So what did I have to do on the first bend? Get a hit on him. That's what I think is the difference between me and him. He likes winning with the fastest car, to drive past everybody and win. Lee Fairhurst is the same. He drives conservatively. Dan Johnson, I think he should win a lot more. It's an aggression thing. Back in the old days, if somebody was quicker than me or Frankie or Andy Smith, we would get them on the first lap to win the race. Mick Sworder does it. Stuart Smith Junior does too. If they want to win a final, they bury everybody on the first bend. They move everybody at the first opportunity. But not everybody does. It's the way it's gone."

Does Speak fear payback from somebody like Harris?

"It's nothing personal. You'll get it back, but because he doesn't drive the same way, it's harder for him to get me than it is for me to get him."

The younger drivers could take a few tips from Speak's style. After all, he's won enough to prove that it works. But perhaps the biggest secret behind his success isn't just his style – it's his whole racing philosophy. He doesn't race to prove anything; he races for enjoyment, the grin firmly fixed under his helmet, constantly smiling and joking in the pits. When he does stop enjoying it, as he has a couple of times in the past, he isn't afraid to walk away. Maybe he'll return with recharged batteries, maybe not. Not that Speak is likely to walk away again anytime soon.

"As long as people are interested in me racing, I'll race," Speak declares. "I just love it."

But he's always been a winner. Could Speak still motivate himself to race as a blue top?

"No. I mean, I might have to. But I don't think other people would be interested."

It's hard to imagine Speak under a blue roof. After all, he's been one of the finest drivers to get behind the wheel of both a Formula 1 and Formula 2. Is he the best racing driver in the history of oval motorsport? It's an argument that will run and run. Is he better than Stuart Smith Senior? Bill Batten? Frankie Wainman Junior? Gordon Moodie? John Lund? Yet one thing is clear. Rob Speak deserves to be known as one of the best drivers in the history of Formula 1 stock car racing.

The ones that got away

Mick Sworder: One of the biggest characters in the sport, Sworder won six meeting finals and nineteen races in total in 2014, the second-highest figures after Tom Harris. But when it came to championship races, luck seemed to elude him and he failed to register on any podiums other than his World Championship Semi-Final. Never afraid to use his front bumper, never afraid to say what he feels, Sworder fears nobody on the racetrack.

Paul Hines: Winner of three meeting finals including two on the trot, Hines may be known as the nice guy but he can still put the bumper in where necessary. A former British and European Champion, Hines has the talent to reach the top step of the podium. Everybody's second-favourite driver won't settle for second place.

Geert-Jan Keijzer: One of the top Dutch drivers, Keijzer was leading the Netherlands-based World Cup until Dan Johnson blasted past. Two months later, Geert-Jan won the Piet Keijzer Memorial Trophy, presented in remembrance of his father – a win which must have meant as much to him as a World Cup win would.

Lee Fairhurst: Former World Champion Fairhurst reverted to mainly racing on his favoured tarmac in 2014. No doubt that harmed his chances to seize the gold roof a second time, although he still finished the World Final one spot off the podium in fourth. Cool and clinical, he'll be one of the favourites next time the World Championship is run on the hard stuff. If he gets out a little more often in his shale car, he'll be one of the favourites every year.

Danny Wainman: Scored more race wins than his big brother for the first time in 2014, but Frankie still beat him to the chequered flag in the European Championship. Alongside Mat Newson, Wainman is one of the best drivers yet to have won a major championship title, but he still has plenty of time on his side.

Ryan Harrison: The pantomime villain of Formula 1 stock cars began the season as holder of the European and National Points Championships but 2014 didn't match up to his previous stellar year. A regular visitor to the disciplinary committee, he ended the year under a cloud and seemingly banned from racing. Some might be glad to see the back of him, but remember: *Stars Wars* would have been boring without Darth Vader.

LIST OF WINNERS

FINAL WINNERS

Sun 23 March	Belle Vue	James Neachell 322
Sat 29 March	King's Lynn	Paul Hines 259
Sat 5 April	Coventry: WCQR	Craig Finnikin 55
Sat 12 April	Birmingham: WCQR	Rob Speak 318
Sun 13 April	Hednesford: WCQR	Rob Speak 318
Fri 18 April	Skegness	Rob Speak 318
Sat 19 April	Stoke: WCQR	Tom Harris 1
Mon 21 April	Belle Vue	Tom Harris 1
Sat 26 April	King's Lynn: WCQR	Mick Sworder 150
Sat 3 May	Coventry	Tom Harris 1
Mon 5 May	Sheffield: WCQR	Paul Hines 259
Sat 10 May	Skegness: WCQR	Paul Hines 259
Sun 11 May	Skegness: UK Open	Stuart Smith Junior 390
Sat 17 May	Birmingham	Luke Davidson 464
Sun 18 May	Buxton: WCQR	Lee Fairhurst 217
Sat 24 May	King's Lynn	Dan Johnson 4
Mon 26 May	Belle Vue: WCQR	Mal Brown 34
Sat 31 May	Northampton	Colin Goodswen 372
Sat 7 June	Coventry	Matt Newson 16
Sat 14 June	Birmingham: British	Paul Harrison 2

Sat 21 June	Ipswich: WCQR	Colin Goodswen 372
Sun 22 June	Northampton: WCQR	Lee Fairhurst 217
Sat 28 June	Cow'bth: WCQR/Scottish	Tom Harris 1
Sun 29 June	Lochgelly: WCQR	Tom Harris 1
Sat 5 July	Coventry	Mick Sworder 150
Sat 12 July	Skegness: U25	Lee Fairhurst 217
Sun 13 July	Skegness	Tom Harris 1
Sat 19 July	Northampton	Tom Harris 1
Sun 20 July	Northampton: European	Lee Fairhurst 217
Sat 26 July	Stoke: World Semi-Final	Dan Johnson 4
Thu 31 July	Skegness	Frankie Wainman Junior 515
Sat 2 Aug	Coventry	Rob Speak 318
Sat 9 Aug	Skegness: World Semi-Final	Lee Fairhurst 217
Sat 16 Aug	King's Lynn	Stuart Smith Junior 390
Mon 25 Aug	Belle Vue: Cons Semi-Final	Frankie Wainman Junior 515
Sat 30 Aug	Birmingham: SO1	Ryan Harrison 197
Sun 31 Aug	Buxton: SO2	Tom Harris 1
Sat 6 Sept	Coventry: SO3	Stuart Smith Junior 390
Fri 19 Sept	Coventry	Pieter Van Der Iest H226
Sat 20 Sept	Coventry: World Final	Mick Sworder 150
Sun 21 Sept	Northampton	Mick Sworder 150
Sat 27 Sept	King's Lynn: SO4	Mick Sworder 150
Sat 4 Oct	Coventry	Mark Woodhull 335
Sat 11 Oct	Skegness: WCQR/SO5	Tom Harris 84
Sun 12 Oct	Belle Vue: WCQR/SO6	Stuart Smith Junior 390
Sat 18 Oct	King's Lynn: WCQR/SO7	Rob Speak 318
Sat 25 Oct	Birmingham: WCQR/SO8	Ivan Pritchard 434
Sun 26 Oct	Northampton: WCQR/SO9	Daniel Van Spijker H231
Sat 1 Nov	Coventry	Mick Sworder 150
Sun 9 Nov	Sheffield: SO10	Timmy Farrell 467
Sat 15 Nov	Birmingham	Paul Ford 388
Sun 28 Dec	Stoke	Tom Harris 84

TOTAL FINAL WINS (5 OR MORE)
1. Tom Harris 1/84 (10)
2. Mick Sworder 150 (6)
3. Rob Speak 318 (5)
=. Lee Fairhurst 217 (5)

TOTAL RACE WINS (10 OR MORE)

1. Tom Harris 1/84 (31)
2. Mick Sworder 150 (19)
3. Dan Johnson 4 (15)
4. Rob Speak 318 (14)
=. Danny Wainman 212 (14)
=. Lee Fairhurst 217 (14)
7. Stuart Smith Junior 390 (13)
8. Frankie Wainman Junior 515 (10)

UK OPEN CHAMPIONSHIP

Sunday 11 May, Skegness
1. Stuart Smith Junior 390
2. Mat Newson 16
3. Tom Harris 1

BRITISH CHAMPIONSHIP

Saturday 14 June, Birmingham
1. Paul Harrison 2
2. Mat Newson 16
3. Paul Ford 388

SCOTTISH CHAMPIONSHIP

Saturday 28 June, Cowdenbeath
1. Tom Harris 1
2. Rob Speak 318
3. Lee Fairhurst 217

UNDER 25 CHAMPIONSHIP

Saturday 12 July, Skegness
1. Tom Harris 1
2. Danny Wainman 212
3. Luke Davidson 464

EUROPEAN CHAMPIONSHIP

Saturday 20 July, Northampton
1. Frankie Wainman Junior 515
2. Danny Wainman 212
3. Mat Newson 16

WORLD CHAMPIONSHIP SEMI-FINALS
Saturday 26 July, Stoke
1. Mat Newson 16
2. Frankie Wainman Junior 515
3. Dan Johnson 4

Saturday 9 August, Skegness
1. Paul Harrison 2
2. Rob Speak 318
3. Mick Sworder 150

WORLD CUP
Sunday 17 August, Venray
1. Dan Johnson UK4
2. Geert-Jan Keijzer 6
3. Lee Robinson 107

WORLD CHAMPIONSHIP
Saturday 20 September, Coventry
1. Craig Finnikin 55
2. Stuart Smith Junior 390
3. Dan Johnson 4
4. Lee Fairhurst 217
5. Frankie Wainman Junior 515
6. Tom Harris 1
7. Paul Hines 259
8. Will Yarrow 22
9. Mal Brown 34
10. Danny Wainman 212

NOVICE OF THE YEAR
1. Will Hunter 220 (291)
2. Karl Roberts 313 (71)
3. Paul-Jay Lemons 444 (51)

GRAND NATIONAL CHAMPIONSHIP
1. Frankie Wainman Junior 515
2. Mat Newson 16
3. Rob Speak 318

NATIONAL POINTS CHAMPIONSHIP
1. Rob Speak 318 (357)
2. Tom Harris 84 (332)
3. Mat Newson 16 (328)
4. Frankie Wainman Junior 515 (310)
5. Mick Sworder 150 (286)
6. Craig Finnikin 55 (277)
7. Danny Wainman 212 (271)
8. Paul Harrison 2 (221)
9. Dan Johnson 4 (190)
10. Paul Hines 259 (136)
11. Lee Fairhurst 217 (74)
12. Luke Davidson 464 (41)

ACKNOWLEDGEMENTS

Who would have thought that, sixty years on from the first meeting at New Cross Stadium in 1954, stock car drivers would still be meeting up at oval tracks to race and crash together? The longevity of Formula 1 stock cars is surely because it is the perfect motorsport for spectators. They can see all the on-track action from the stands without relying on big screens; they can see the off-the-track action in the pits too – you don't get that in the other F1! The best drivers have to pass the slower ones on their way to victory, so overtaking is guaranteed. Contact is allowed, so being the best doesn't rely solely on having a good car. Some might worry about growing costs, but stock car racing is still one of the most inclusive and accessible forms of motorsport there is.

I wanted to mark the sixtieth season of F1 stock cars in some way. Others are more qualified to write about the rich history of the sport, so I wanted to look at the contemporary scene. But the biggest problem was which drivers to include and which to not. It was always going to be a hard choice – I didn't want to ignore those who deserved inclusion, but I was aware that it was going to be impossible to feature everybody and keep the book manageable.

About halfway through the 2014 season, I realised that most of the championships were being won by different drivers – no one driver was dominating. Once Craig Finnikin picked up the World title, I began hoping that the silver roof would go to somebody different again. Thankfully, Rob Speak helped out by taking that one! So, the format was set: *Kings of the Oval* would be based around the championship winners of the 2014 season.

That meant a few big names missed out: Mick Sworder, Paul Hines, Geert-Jan Keijzer, Lee Fairhurst, Danny Wainman and Ryan Harrison. I could easily have found three more to make a completely different book. Maybe that will be next year's project!

Thankfully, all of the drivers who were featured were happy to give up their time to be interviewed, answering my many and occasionally difficult questions openly and with good grace. To the drivers: thank you very much, this book would not have been possible without your help.

All of the drivers who race in Formula 1 stock cars are helped out by friends and family who keep them on track and winning. I can't possibly list them all on their behalf, but rest assured that if you provide help with a spanner, if you open your wallet as a sponsor, if you are a family member or friend who provides moral support – it is vastly appreciated by the drivers. And if you are a fan who cheers from the sidelines or exchanges a quick word with your favourite in the pits, that's much appreciated too!

Some might say that this book is a shameless copy of Neil Randon's *The Sound and the Fury*, published in 2000. I'd have to disagree and state unequivocally that this book is based entirely on *Keep Turning Left* instead. The only trouble is that *Keep Turning Left* was itself a shameless copy of *The Sound and the Fury*! In all seriousness, *The Sound and the Fury* is a stock car classic and I thoroughly recommend you beg, borrow or steal a copy. An interesting footnote is that of the nine drivers Neil interviewed for *The Sound and the Fury*, three are also featured in *Kings of the Oval*: Paul Harrison, Frankie Wainman Junior and Rob Speak. That says something about the longevity of some of the Formula 1 greats.

John Lund was also featured in *The Sound and the Fury* and he was a natural choice to provide the foreword to this book. When John first rolled out on track as a white top – and a pretty chaotic one at that – I hadn't even been born. 38 years on, he is still mixing it with the best. Long may that continue!

One thing that Neil Randon wasn't able to make full use of at the turn of the millennium was the internet. How times change. Fourteen years later, I couldn't even think about researching anything without it. Two websites have been particularly useful in putting together this book. Firstly, f1stockcars.com is a brilliant fan site and showpiece for the sport. Frankly, it puts the official websites to shame. Secondly, briscaf1stox.co.uk is the ultimate statistical resource for anybody interested in Formula 1 stock car history. However, I warn you to be careful before you type in that address – you'll find yourself cruising the links for hours and hours!

Colin Casserley provided the majority of the photographs. As well as being the premier F1 paparazzi, he puts in a huge amount of work behind the scenes to support oval motorsport in the media. Colin responded promptly to all my requests, never getting frustrated with my regular additions to the long list of required photos. At least, if he did, he didn't show it! Thanks also to Kevin Wickham, who plugged the F2 gap, and Mike Greenwood, whose selection of historic photos is brilliant.

Eddie, Mark and Marcus – the cheerful EdCreations trio – sell my books at many stock car meetings. Nobody typifies the friendly stock car community more than these three chaps. Over the last decade, thousands of young boys and girls have dreamed of the chequered flag while playing with their EdCreation model stock cars. Whether any of those kids have grown up and driven an F1 is currently unknown, but the models certainly help to keep the young generation interested. Thanks guys, and sorry for regularly messing up the 1p system!

Thanks also go to Gary Reeves for technical advice and picking up typos and discrepancies in the early drafts of this book, and I must also thank my wife, Roisin, not only for proof reading, but for her all-round support. We're both spectacularly pleased that our first child will be born at some point during the 2015 stock car season. Perhaps the baby will be named after a Formula 1 stock car legend – you might spot young Frankie Reeves or Stuart Reeves around the racetrack fairly soon. I'm pretty sure Roisin won't allow me to name it after the current dominant force in F2. After all, Moodie Reeves doesn't quite sound right!

To buy copies of the images in this book go to

Also from Chequered Flag Publishing

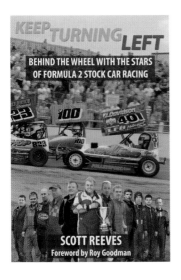

KEEP TURNING LEFT

by Scott Reeves
foreword by Roy Goodman

Success in the world of Formula 2 stock car racing takes a rare combination of aggression, skill and luck. Only the best drivers get to race under the gold roof of the World Champion.

In *Keep Turning Left*, twelve top F2 drivers give an open and honest account of racing bumper to bumper in full contact motorsport. They reveal their highs and lows, their motivations and frustrations, their joys and regrets.

With over 100 colour photographs and intimate access to the drivers, this is a must-read book for every follower of Formula 2 stock car racing.

A proportion of the price of this book will be donated to the BriSCA F2 Benevolent Fund.

GOLD TOP
The John Lund Story

by Scott Reeves
foreword by Paul Hines

In 1987, John Lund's eleven year struggle behind the wheel finally came good – he won the stock car World Final. Little did he realise that over twenty years later he would still be part of the sport, having won the World Final more times than any other.

Gold Top tells the story behind John Lund's stock car career. Based on interviews with John and his family, it draws the rich anecdotes from a quiet and modest champion to conjure a colourful and compelling biography.

From triumph to tragedy, this is the long journey that made John Lund one of the most experienced, popular and successful drivers in the history of motorsport.

A proportion of the price of this book will be donated to the British Stock Car Drivers Association Benevolent Fund.

Also from Chequered Flag Publishing

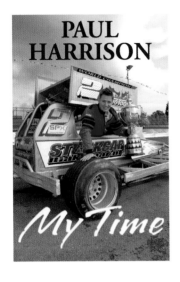

My Time
by Paul Harrison

"I just feel that my time has come."

When Paul Harrison uttered those words before the Formula 1 Stock Car World Final in 2011, he was about to make history. It was the culmination of a life spent trying to match his father's achievement and wear the gold roof that signifies the World Champion.

Paul Harrison tells the story of his year as World Champion, revealing the determination and willpower that is required to remain at the top of stock car racing. From the exhilaration of victory to the pressure of performing under the gold roof, *My Time* is a unique behind-the-scenes account of this brutal motorsport.